Better Small Talk:
Talk to Anyone, Avoid Awkwardness, Generate Deep Conversations, and Make Real Friends

By Patrick King
Social Interaction and Conversation Coach at
www.PatrickKingConsulting.com

Table of Contents

BETTER SMALL TALK: *TALK TO ANYONE, AVOID AWKWARDNESS, GENERATE DEEP CONVERSATIONS, AND MAKE REAL FRIENDS*   1

TABLE OF CONTENTS   3

CHAPTER 1. UGH, SMALL TALK   5

THE SMALL TALK MINDSET   9
A CHILDLIKE EXERCISE   18
YOUR CONVERSATION RÉSUMÉ   26
CONVERSATIONAL STAGES   33

CHAPTER 2. INITIAL IMPRESSIONS   43

SET THE TONE   46
MAKE THE FIRST MOVE   53
FIND SIMILARITY   60
MANUFACTURE CONNECTION   70

CHAPTER 3. HOW TO BE CAPTIVATING   80

A LIFE OF STORIES   82
THE 1:1:1 METHOD   89
THE STORY SPINE   94
INSIDE STORIES   103
ASK FOR STORIES   107

CHAPTER 4. KEEP IT FLOWING AND SMOOTH   119

CREATE MOTION   120
THINK ON YOUR FEET   131
HELPFUL ACRONYMS   139

CHAPTER 5. GO DEEPER, BE BETTER   153

THE OLDEST TRICK IN THE BOOK   154
TWO EARS, ONE MOUTH   161
ASK BETTER QUESTIONS   174

CHAPTER 6. LOOKING INWARDS   189

BUILD THYSELF   192
BRANCH OUT   197
YOU ONLY SEE BLACK AND WHITE   202

SUMMARY GUIDE   213

Chapter 1. Ugh, Small Talk

Human beings are a social species. Connection is crucial to happiness, staving off depression, and keeping healthy—literally. Various studies have shown that the effects of loneliness are akin to eating a poorer diet and exercising less, and can ultimately lead to the same place—an early death.

It might sound a little melodramatic, but companionship is literally the way our brains have been built to survive and thrive. In fact, many evolutionary biologists now accept the theory that humans developed their higher-order thinking abilities specifically *because* they lived in complex social groups. The existence of language, empathy, and maybe even culture itself comes down to the fact that humans have, since the very beginning, lived and worked together.

But for the purposes of this book's topic, there's an even more important wrinkle: the *quality* of our interactions matters as well, not just the quantity or presence of other people around us. If your kneejerk reaction is "ugh, small talk," you might not be alone. As anyone with a large, chaotic family can tell you, not every social interaction is beneficial or carried out with a purpose. And if you have dozens of "friends" you wouldn't dare talk honestly with, you probably also understand the quality/quantity dilemma.

In fact, it even sounds like even our brains despise small talk. A 2010 study by Matthias Mehl had participants wandering around in their daily lives armed with a device that would record their audio environment over three days. The researchers analyzed how long each participant was in the presence of other people, and whether they were having casual conversations or were talking about more substantive matters. Basically, the aim was to capture what kinds of interactions these participants were taking part in, and the effect they had on their lives.

At the same time, the researchers also measured people's overall level of happiness and mental and physical well-being. They found a clear correlation between substantive and deep discussions and greater well-being and happiness. It's something you've probably suspected or even felt before, but being vulnerable and open with others is a deeply satisfying activity on many levels.

As for small talk, that which is the opposite of substance and depth? Well, it drew a negative correlation with well-being and happiness, meaning it made people *less* happy. The research suggested it was "big talk" that was responsible for all those beneficial effects we're always being told come with socializing.

There you have it; real evidence that small talk is something to be avoided, or at least transition out of as quickly as possible.

Researcher Arthur Aron conducted a study in 1997, in which he paired participants who didn't know each other and gave them a list of fairly personal questions to ask. Although the questions were not offensively intrusive, they were more than just small talk. ("Would you like to be famous and how?" "Do you have a secret hunch about how you will die?" "What is your most terrible memory?" "How do you feel about your relationship with your mother?")

Aron found that the participants responded to these "deep dives" with openness and intimacy. The participants didn't feel that the questions, as personal as they were, necessarily invaded their privacy or weakened them in any way. Instead, these questions encouraged honesty, more emotional fluency, and sincerity in the respondents. They felt closer to the other participants, who were complete strangers before the experiment. Future iterations of this study were given names such as "How to fall in love with 36 questions" because of the powerful effects it had on the relationships between the participants, which were previously nonexistent.

You probably already know deep in your bones what these two studies laid out: delving more deeply or intensely in our communications can create positive results far more swiftly than one might think. Now the question remains: how can we actually do that? In this book, I want to provide a framework, from beginning to end, about how to engage people more effectively and move beyond small talk. We'll start even before the interaction begins with how you should prepare yourself, and move on through all the stages of small talk to arrive at something more meaningful.

At the prospect of reading this book, you might be overly excited about throwing yourself into the midst of a conversation and seeing what you can accomplish. After all, you're reading this book for a reason, and motivation can make you overeager—but rushing in would be a mistake for the time being. It would be akin to running into battle without your shield, sword, or even pants.

The Small Talk Mindset

There's more to conversation than thinking off the cuff and creating witty banter out of nothing at all. Very few of us are capable of doing that on a consistent basis, and what's more sustainable, easy, and practical is preparing for a conversation beforehand.

To be specific, you're not preparing for specific conversations like they are job interviews—rather, you are priming yourself to be able to shine in social exchanges in general. There's a distinct difference between the two. Don't worry about appearing forced or tackling the problem in a serious and overly formal way. Though it might seem counterintuitive, preparing well and making deliberate efforts to perform better in natural conversation can actually make you *more* spontaneous and relaxed. When you prepare for conversations, you'll find being witty much more available and even easy.

So the first step to witty banter and small talk is to get ready psychologically—so you're not caught with your pants down in meeting someone new. What exactly does this mean? Think about when you just wake up and your voice is gravelly and incomprehensible. Your thoughts are unorganized and swirling, and anything that comes out of your mouth is likely to be responded to with a "...what did you say?"

When you're only half-awake, you're caught off guard when you have to respond to anything, and you have a lack of focus and awareness. This is our social status quo— how we normally move through and navigate the world. So warming up mentally is about beginning to stretch and gingerly flex our social muscles so we're ready for action.

If you're out at a bar or networking event, you only have one shot at making the right impression. If you fall flat on your face, as will inevitably happen from time to time, guess what? That was your one shot at the goal— will you make the most of it?

Recall that as children, we were always

admonished to never talk to strangers. This well-meaning instruction might have served us well in our childhood, when we were likely to be gullible prey to sly criminals. *Stranger danger* was a real thing to be avoided.

In public places, we plug our ears with headphones and glue our faces to our phones, preferring to keep our interactions with people we don't know to the bare minimum. Is this habit still serving us well? Likely not if our goal is to become better at conversation and charm. We should quickly let go of this tendency because, as adults, it only serves to keep us isolated from others. It locks us in a social prison of our own making, and it keeps us socially cold for occasions when we need to be *on*. At the very least, it leaves us woefully unprepared for engaging with people, exposed as if we were ambushed in the middle of the night.

A 2014 study by Epley and Schroeder divided commuters on trains and buses into three groups—the first was instructed to interact with a stranger near them, the second to keep to themselves, and the third to commute as normal. Even though participants in each group predicted feeling more positive if they kept to themselves, the outcome of the experiment was the opposite. At the end of their ride, the group of commuters who connected with a stranger reported a more positive experience than those who remained disconnected. It seems we feel that only awkwardness will ensue with a stranger, when instead an unexpected connection creates good vibrations.

In support of the above findings, another study by Sandstrom and Dunn (2013) revealed how being our usual, efficiency-driven selves while buying our daily cup of coffee is robbing us of an opportunity to be happier. While we routinely rush through the transaction without so much as a smile, the study found that people who smiled and engaged in a brief conversation with the barista experienced more positive feelings than those who stuck to the impersonal, efficient approach.

These studies have two main findings. First, we tend to *think* or *assume* we're better off keeping to ourselves than having short interactions with strangers. Second, we're wrong about the first point. The simple act of engaging people in short bursts has been shown to make us happier and more inclined to be social, and it will also help us mentally and psychologically warm up to be our best in conversations and small talk no matter the context.

There seems to be a question of inertia. As we go through our days, we're typically a little caught up in our own heads, or distracted with whatever we're doing. It's as though the default setting is to be turned "off" socially. What does this tell us? That if we want to become more sociable, master the art of conversation, make more friends or simply be that person who can easily make people laugh and like them, then we need to find a way to move ourselves out of this antisocial mode. We need to become more comfortable and skilled at being "on" socially—a bit like a well-trained athlete might find it easier to start running than someone who hasn't run for years!

We need to engage in more short interactions—or what researcher Steven Handel calls "ten-second relationships"—with others, because they have the potential to boost our moods, change our perspectives, and warm us up socially. It's as though these interactions keep the social engagement engine running.

Of course, though we may now recognize the benefits of short interactions, it's still understandable how the thought of striking up a conversation with a total stranger may be uninviting or even repulsive to those of us who aren't social butterflies. We feel ill-equipped to engage in fruitful social interactions, so we prefer the loneliness of keeping to ourselves.

But if this is your knee-jerk response to approaching people cold or striking up conversations with strangers, just remind yourself that you have a natural bias to assume that you prefer keeping to yourself. You can probably recall a situation where you were glad you reached out and engaged with someone, even if you were reluctant at first. A lot of people hate small talk simply because shifting gears into socializing mode can feel awkward or uncomfortable. But they forget that, once warmed up, the benefits far outweigh the initial costs. It's a bit like exercise in the morning. Sure, it takes your muscles time to warm up, but you soon start to enjoy yourself, and gain the benefits of physical activity.

How do we counter our natural tendency to avoid small interactions and warm ourselves up for routinely conversing with others? How do we get into the habit of being interested in people and build enough social confidence so we can turn that interest into meaningful interactions?

Well, that's part of the logic behind only trying for ten-second interactions. Hey, you can make it one second (*Hello there!*) or five seconds (*Hi, how's your day going? Great to hear, bye!*) depending on your level of comfort. But keep the goal small and stay consistent.

You constantly encounter multiple opportunities for warming up to interactions and building your social confidence. For instance, think of your typical day. On your way to work, how many people do you spend at least some time ignoring—whether those you pass by on the street, sit with on your commute, or stand beside in elevators? Greet at least one of those people with "*Good morning*" and offer either a compliment ("*Nice coat. The fabric looks cozy.*"), an observation ("*The sky's cloudless today. Looks like the showers are letting up.*"), or a question ("*I see you're reading John Grisham. Which of his novels is your favorite?*").

For lunch, do you eat solo, hunched over your work desk? Try instead to spend your lunch hour someplace with shared seating, such as your office pantry or a nearby picnic area. Sit beside a colleague you always see in your building yet never got the chance to talk to, and get the conversation rolling by asking about recent company events ("*I heard your department is starting a new leg of research. How's it going?*").

Finally, as you pick up groceries on your way home, chat with another shopper mulling over products in the same grocery aisle you're in ("*I saw this sauce in an online recipe. Have you tried cooking with it?*").

At the checkout counter, smile and greet the cashier ("*How's your shift going so far?*"). This segment of society is especially suited to help you practice and warm up—in fact, they don't really have much of a choice. Baristas. Cab drivers. Cashiers. The grocery bag boy. Waiters. Doormen. Valets.

Their job performance depends on their customer service skills, and if they want to keep their jobs, they have to be courteous to you. This alone should eliminate the fear you have of crashing and burning in any social interaction, because it's their job to prevent that and probably laugh at your jokes. You'll see that crashing and burning is never really that bad, and people move on quickly—they'll probably forget the interaction within the next ten minutes.

There's also typically a captive audience behind the store counter or cash register. These employees are usually stuck being stationary in a position for long periods of time, and for those who have held the above jobs... you know that it's not the most thrilling life. Most of the time, they are bored out of their minds, so having someone engage them will be a positive experience for them. You will make their day pass faster and just give them something to do. You might be the only one to treat them with respect and show actual interest in them as a person, which would undoubtedly make you the highlight of their day. In other words, they'll be glad to talk to you.

With service people, you can test different stories, reactions, phrases, greetings, facial expressions, and so on. Unless you offend them in a deeply personal way, these people will still be courteous to you, but you can gauge how positive their reactions are to all of your tactics to know what works best. You can continuously improve and hone your skills. You can witness your progress with future interactions. As you see their reactions change, you can fine-tune what you're doing and keep stepping up your game.

Essentially, you're in a *safe environment to practice and polish your social skills* without fear of any judgment or consequences. More than that, you can learn to read people, process their signals, and calibrate your interactions to different types of people. This is a process that takes trial and error, but you can speed it up exponentially by engaging with the people you come across.

So make it a goal to initiate and create a ten-second interaction with a stranger each day, and especially on the way to functions, events, and parties. This will warm you up for conversation and build the habit of being interested in people.

A Childlike Exercise

Warming yourself up psychologically and getting into the general mood to socialize on a daily basis are important aspects of being great at small talk, but just as important is the way you prepare your body. Think of it this way: conversation is a race, and you have to warm up and prepare yourself accordingly.

When we want our best race, whether athletic or academic, we always engage in some type of warm-up. It's almost common sense at this point that you need to prime your body and mind to the kind of performance that you want. Runners stretch, singers sing scales. What about people engaging in conversation?

Well, you might be surprised by how much help your speaking muscles need and how getting them in shape can make you instantly more charismatic. Recall back in grade school when you weren't paying attention, the teacher called on you, and you had to spend five seconds clearing your throat while still sounding meek and awkward because you weren't prepared. That's what we are seeking to eliminate, as well as imbuing you with a sense of confidence.

To warm up your conversation and small talk skills, you just need to do something we've done almost every day in our lives: **read out loud**.

It sounds simple, but reading out loud this time will be different from any other it because you will have a purpose. I've provided an excerpt from the *Wizard of Oz*, which is in the public domain—for those copyright police out there. If this doesn't pique your interest, you can feel free to find your own excerpt. Just try to make sure there is a multitude of emotions included, preferably with dialogue from different characters. Here it is:

> *After climbing down from the china wall the travelers found themselves in a disagreeable country, full of bogs and marshes and covered with tall, rank grass. It was difficult to walk without falling into muddy holes, for the grass was so thick that it hid them from sight.*
>
> *However, by carefully picking their way, they got safely along until they reached solid ground. But here the country seemed wilder than ever, and after a long and tiresome walk through the underbrush they entered another forest, where the trees were bigger and older than any they had ever seen.*
>
> *"This forest is perfectly delightful," declared the Lion, looking around him with joy. "Never have I seen a more beautiful place."*
>
> *"It seems gloomy," said the Scarecrow.*
>
> *"Not a bit of it," answered the Lion. "I should like to live here all my life. See how soft the dried leaves are under your feet and how rich and green the moss is*

that clings to these old trees. Surely no
wild beast could wish a pleasanter
home."

"Perhaps there are wild beasts in the
forest now," said Dorothy.

"I suppose there are," returned the Lion,
"but I do not see any of them about."

They walked through the forest until it
became too dark to go any farther.
Dorothy and Toto and the Lion lay
down to sleep, while the Woodman and
the Scarecrow kept watch over them as
usual.

Seems like an easy task, right? Go ahead and
try to read the above excerpt out loud to
yourself. Don't be shy. If you actually did it,
you'll notice that you do literally feel warmed
up and more ready to keep speaking and
conversing after just using your vocal cords
for a bit. When you feel physically warmed
up, it's easier to feel more psychologically and
socially ready, too. But that's just the
beginning. Now comes the instruction.

Pretend like you are reading the excerpt out
loud to a class of second graders. Read the
excerpt like you're giving a performance in a

contest, and the winner is judged on how emotional and ridiculous they can be! Pretend you're a voice actor for a movie trailer and you have only your voice to convey a wide range of emotion. Go as far over the top as possible—which, granted, won't be much at first.

Exaggerate every emotion you can find to the tenth degree. Scream parts of the story while whispering in other parts. Use different and zany voices for different characters. Make any laughter maniacal, make any rage boiling, make any happiness manic—you get the idea. For that matter, what emotions are you picking up in the text? Even in such a short excerpt, there are emotional high and low points. Express them, and make them sound like climaxes to stretch your range of emotion.

Pay attention to your voice tonality. Are you accustomed to using a monotone? Would someone be able to tell what the character or narrator is thinking or trying to convey by listening to you? Use the excerpt to practice your range of vocal expressiveness—try to embody the term *emotional diversity*. Go ahead and try it for the second time with all this newfound instruction.

Did you hear a difference? Here is some additional instruction: pay attention to your diction and how you enunciate. In a sense, you are literally warming your tongue up so you don't stutter or stumble on your words when you talk to others. This is another reason to have an excerpt with dialogue—the greater the diversity of the text you are reading, the better warmed up you will be. If you have the habit of muttering like a curmudgeon, put a stop to it and make sure you are speaking clear as a bell.

Pay attention to your breathing. Do you feel like you're running out of breath? It's because your diaphragm is weak and not used to projecting or sounding confident. That's the reason singers put their hands on their stomachs—it's to check that their diaphragms are engaged. Try it and make sure that your stomach is taut and tight. Become aware of how much air you're pulling into your body, and how you're spending that air on the words as you say them.

The point here is to literally breathe life into the words that you are speaking. Those who speak without their diaphragm inevitably come off as quiet, meek, and mouse-like. The better you can project your voice, the wider the emotional range you can create. Your breathing, your vocal expression and your emotions are all tightly connected. If you're nervous, your breathing becomes shallow and your voice shakes. But it works the other way round, too: if you can master your breathing and voice, you may find it a little easier to conquer your nervous emotions.

Another key element of how you say something is, of course, your pacing—the speed at which you talk. Your speaking speed can either be your friend or undermine what you're trying to say. Rate of speech can imply an emotion all by itself—for instance, when making a big point, you should slow your pace to allow the impact to be felt. If you use the wrong speed or your pacing is off, a lot of what you have to say can easily be lost or confused and misinterpreted. In addition, well-timed pauses can say just as much as an expression through words.

Ready to read through the excerpt one more time? Make sure you're utilizing everything you just read. Now compare your third version to the first version you did without any instruction. *That's* the difference between warming yourself up and not, and most likely, the first version is how you're coming across the vast majority of the time. Hopefully that's illustrative enough evidence for the benefits of warming up.

More than that, it might show you something else: that being lively and engaging in social situations is not necessarily natural or easy for anyone. It does take a little effort, and it does take some time to ease into it. Sometimes, people who want to improve their social skills mistakenly think there's something wrong with them for not finding it easier. But even naturally outgoing and extroverted people need to warm up in this way!

Was this exercise, along with all the included direction, a massive challenge for you? It's probably a good idea to evaluate how unexpressive you are coming off in everyday conversations. You have seen how different your own expression can be in the first round compared to the third. Isn't it an interesting thought, that a friendly, outgoing, confident version of yourself exists just a little preparation away?

If you want to, you could try variations on this exercise. Some people might warm up on their drive over to a party by singing loudly in the car. They deepen and regulate their breathing, practice expressive speaking, and give their mood and confidence a boost at the same time. It may sound cheesy, but you can get the same effect by doing an energetic dance in your room, or talking to a mirror. You get your blood pumping, you lift your energy, and bring focus to your expression, both verbal and nonverbal.

The added bonus is that while you are feeling silly and over the top, you are actually stretching your limits in terms of emotional and vocal expressiveness. The simple act of getting out of your comfort zone, even in private, will extend your boundaries and make you more expressive and confident-sounding in general. All this from reading out aloud? Yes, if done with purpose and deliberation!

Your Conversation Résumé

Previous points in this chapter about pre-conversation have centered around your psychology and your physiology. In other words, to hit the ground running and have great small talk, you've got to find ways to put yourself in the mood for it. However, we haven't covered what to actually say yet, have we? Now we'll rectify that.

As mentioned before, conversation isn't always about thinking quickly on your feet in the heat of the moment. That's an entirely different skill that can be developed, but what's more easy and useful on a daily basis is to create for yourself a *conversation résumé,* which you can draw from in nearly every conversation.

What the heck does this mean? Well, a couple of things.

First, we don't really think about ourselves and what is interesting about us to others. Have you ever played the game "two truths and a lie"? It's a social ice-breaking game where you are supposed to name interesting facts and stories about yourself—but this is pretty difficult for most of us because we simply don't often ask ourselves, *What do people want to hear about us*? Constructing this resume helps confirm your identity, quirks, accomplishments, and unique perspectives; in fact, it helps us gain self-awareness and self-confidence.

Second, when we're in the heat of a conversation and an awkward silence is looming, sometimes we stress and our minds blank completely. We try to think on our feet, but our feet are frozen to the floor. A conversation résumé comes to the rescue because it is an annotated overview of who you are. It's a brief list of your best and funniest stories, your notable accomplishments, your unique experiences, and viewpoints on salient and topical issues. It allows you to keep your best bits ready for usage.

It's no different from a résumé you would use for a job interview—but with a very different purpose in mind here. Know your personal talking points, rehearse them, and be ready to unleash them whenever necessary. However, just like in a job interview, having this résumé allows you to present the version of yourself that you most want others to see.

It may seem inconsequential to have such thoughts prepared, but imagine how excruciating the silence is in a job interview when you have to scramble, think of an answer on the fly, and respond while knowing your words are generic or useless. If someone asks you what your biggest flaw is, you won't have to grasp for straws, and instead can begin expounding on why the fact that you are *too* dedicated and work *too* hard can be a flaw.

It's the difference between having a good answer or story when someone asks, "What did you do last weekend?" versus simply saying, "Oh, not too much. Some TV. What about you?" And how few of us can answer the following without stuttering and stalling: "So what's your story?" The conversation résumé allows you to remind yourself that you're not such a boring person after all, and that people should have reason to be interested in you and what you have to say.

Developing and constantly updating your conversation résumé can save you from awkward silences and make it nearly effortless to connect with others. It may feel difficult to come up with right now, but imagine how much easier it will be without the stress of someone staring at you, waiting for your reply. It's this process of mental agony that will translate to real conversational success.

What you come up with on your résumé won't always make it into everyday conversation, but the more you have it on your brain, the more it will be apparent to others, and the more captivating you will become. A great side effect is that if you know you are ready and prepped ahead of time, you can relax a little more, and this will only help you appear (and feel!) more confident in the moment.

There are four sections to your conversation résumé, and it's not a bad idea to update them every couple of weeks. Admittedly, you may never have thought to answer any of these questions before, which means these parts of you definitely aren't coming through in conversation. Don't sell yourself short!

To be more comfortable in social situations, it's a great idea to make the subtle shift in perspective and imagine how you appear to others, from their point of view. Many of us are so stuck in our own heads, we lose sight of the fact that people only know us in so far as we can share ourselves with them directly. Many times, we think we're so much more boring than we really are!

Keep in mind that if someone asks you a question, you don't have to answer them literally, and instead can redirect them to something else that you've prepared on your conversation résumé. After all, when someone asks "How was your weekend?" they don't necessarily want to know about the weekend, they just want to hear something entertaining to fill the silence.

Daily life:
- What did you do over the weekend? Anything notable?

- How is your week/day going? Anything notable?
- How is your family/significant other? Anything notable?
- How is work going? Anything notable?

Personal:
- What are your hobbies? Anything notable?
- What's your biggest passion or interest outside of work? Anything notable?
- Where are you from? Anything notable?
- How long have you lived at your current location and worked at your current job? Anything notable?
- Where did you go to school and what subjects and activities were you involved in? Anything notable?
- What do you do for work? Anything notable?

Notable:
- What are your five most unique experiences?
- What are your five most personally significant accomplishments?
- What are ten strengths—things you are above average at, no matter how big or small.
- Name ten places you have traveled in the past five years.

- Name the past five times you have gone out to a social event.
- Name ten things you cannot live without—don't take this question too literally. It is asking about your interests, not household staples.

Staying Current:
- What are the top five current events of the week *and* month? Learn the basics and develop an opinion and stance on them.
- What are four funny personal situations from the past week? Be able to summarize them as a brief story.
- What are the four most interesting things you've read or heard about in the past week? Be able to summarize them as a brief story.

If you've ever felt like your mind was going blank, this is the cure. There are so many pieces of information that you've just dug out of yourself that it should be nearly impossible to run out of things to say. Remember to review this résumé before you head into socially intense situations, and you will be able to keep up with just about anyone.

You just may realize that while some people appear to be quicker than lightning, they may simply remember more about themselves at that moment.

Conversational Stages

Look, small talk gets a bad rap. You yourself may find the whole topic kind of boring or unpleasant. But failing to understand the value of small talk is like saying you want to be married but hate dating—one typically leads to the other in a very sequential manner. In the beginning of this chapter we noted that the conversational first prize is deep, meaningful interaction with others. But, the only way to get there is to become masterful at small talk, first.

The first thing to remember, then, when attempting to improve your social skills, is that small talk has a very important place in the art of conversation, and mastering it will get you to the "big" talk a lot faster. No, small talk in itself is not a life-or-death skill to acquire. But, we would be foolish to disregard it entirely and assume that if we value deep conversation, we can forget about small talk altogether. The opposite is true!

Conversation, and by extension socializing and cultivating relationships with people, is something that happens by degrees, not all at once. Zoom out and you can see where small talk fits in and why it's so important—it's the first of many steps in closing the distance between you and another person.

It can be useful to think of conversations as occurring through four different stages, each one progressively more intimate. By gradually securing trust and rapport with a person, you're more likely to lay the foundation for a good relationship. Similarly, race through these steps or get them wrong and you may well get off on the wrong foot, and ruin a potentially good connection with someone.

The first level is, no surprise, small talk, also known as exchanging pleasantries or general chitchat. This is getting a conversation off the ground from a cold start. It *needs* to be small. Conversational warmup should center around a topic that everyone will be able to comfortably engage with. After all, at this point you don't know the person in front of you at all.

If you waltzed up to a stranger who might become a great friend with time, and proceeded to share a deeply personal story with them with no warning and warm-up, you would have the opposite effect you're hoping for—distancing rather than intimacy.

So, small talk is more or less a question of timing, and of comfortable pacing.

Weather, very general current events or something that is happening in the moment are all good topics. This stage is not about sharing who you are per se, but making contact, and starting things off on a positive foot. Avoid anything too intense or specific, prolonged eye contact or physical touch. Keep it light and smile. Your goal is to *comfortably* move along to the next stage.

Following small talk, you may both feel relaxed enough for the second step: fact disclosure.

This is a "getting to know you" phase where you can start sharing details of your life— where you work or live, interests, what you're doing at the moment, or something that connects to the previous small talk or the position you both find yourselves in currently. You get the chance here to open up a little more and share yourself as a person, which allows trust and confidence to build. However, keep in mind that this is *fact* disclosure—keep strong opinions and emotions out of the picture for now.

Let the other person get to know you

gradually, and only increase intensity if they are comfortable and are responding to your disclosures with their own. If not, it's OK, just stay at this level. If they return your information with some information about themselves, you can likely move along to the next stage.

The third stage—opinion disclosure—brings you both closer still.

Finding common ground allows you to share viewpoints and opinions. Finding what makes both of you the same is a deliberate attempt to seek out grounds for friendship. Without prying, ask thoughtful questions that will let you find a potential area of similarity.

You may need to chat for a while to stumble upon some shared reference of common opinion, but it doesn't necessarily have to be a massive connection. If you've done your small talk well, and you've disclosed some useful facts about yourself (and listened to what you've been told in turn) you can start to find interesting points of commonality to discuss.

Did you study a similar subject at university, do you both have kids, or do you share an unusual interest?

The context of your conversation will determine how in-depth you go. A random chat to an interesting stranger at a bus stop is likely to be a little more shallow than meeting your sister's new fiancé. But the steps will be the same. Good conversationalists know how to keep their ears pricked for facts and details they can draw on or ask questions about. People can be really fascinating if you only ask them the right questions!

Be aware, however, that if you haven't been too successful at the previous stages, seeking out a shared connection might feel a bit forward or unwelcome if the other person wants to move more slowly. You may accidentally uncover a source of friction, and you need to be able to fall back on some good rapport and friendliness from the previous stages.

Conversation is a fine balance—you want to connect with others but need to stay respectful and observant, and maintain a comfortable distance as you get to know the other person. Simply understand that opening up honestly to another person takes time and trust, since it could lead to plenty of discomfort or misunderstanding. Move on to the third stage only if the conversation feels relaxed and positive.

The final stage of emotion disclosure is where you open up even further and share personal feelings directly. This has to be genuine. Everyone has different thresholds for this level of intimacy, so it's important that conversation partners are both authentically trusting and comfortable with one another— hence all the previous stages! You might talk about something you're excited or fearful about, or share a sincere compliment or private opinion.

Of course, a good relationship will stay in this final stage and deepen when it comes to mutually sharing emotions and more vulnerable ideas. Whether it's a romantic, business or family bond, getting to this stage takes effort, and is not to be taken for granted. Though small talk might seem like a waste of time to some, think of it more like a commitment to laying the early foundations of a closer relationship down the line.

Takeaways:

- We are a social species, and multiple studies confirm this. Lack of social interaction itself is harmful, and for our purposes, lack of *substantive* social interaction is no better. Gaining the ability and skill to fast-forward through small talk has incredible value for the relationships in your life—old and future. However, before we jump into conversation tactics, it's helpful to start before we actually meet and greet someone. How can we prepare beforehand to have consistently great small talk and interactions? In many ways, it turns out.

- There are a couple of ways we can get ready for small talk and warm up, so to speak. The two approaches are what you might assume: physiologically, and psychologically. Psychological preparation is a matter of getting in the mood to socialize and also becoming used to initiating interaction. This can be done with "ten-second relationships," which plunge you into the deep end if only for a moment. The idea is to start small and short, with low expectations, and build from there. You'll eventually see that it's easy and quite safe—you might even find it to be enjoyable, and frequently want to extend past ten seconds.
- Physically, you should seek to warm up by reading out loud before socializing and making sure you exaggerate emotional expressiveness and variation. Read a

passage out loud three times and notice the difference in engagement, and you can instantly see the contrast in how you might come across. You should act like a teacher reading to grade school-aged children, and run through the whole gamut of emotions, expressions, and voices. Go over the top. This is meant to warm you up, as well as bring awareness to how lacking in expressiveness you probably are on a normal basis.

- An additional way of preparing before conversations is to get your own information and life in order, and this can be done by following a conversation résumé. The purpose is to draw into your past and find what makes you an interesting person, and make sure that is all at the tip of your tongue for easy usage. We often forget what we can bring to a conversation, and this lack of available topics adds a sense of stress and avoidance.

- We all dislike small talk, but it does have a role. Getting to know someone happens in a sequential manner, and we cannot skip steps if we want to go deeper. It can be said that there are four stages to an interaction, and small talk is the first, followed by fact disclosure, then opinion disclosure, then emotion disclosure. The sequence can be played with, but understanding small talk's role is important.

Chapter 2. Initial Impressions

Most people don't barrel into conversation headfirst – that is, if they don't want to come across as uncomfortably intense or rude. Rather, they gently dip a toe in and test the waters. They extend a little gesture or idea toward the other person, then gauge the response, then adjust according to that response, bit by bit. If you've never met someone before, you naturally feel like you should first remain reserved so you can calibrate your interactions, read your new acquaintance, and determine how familiar or relaxed you can be.

For instance, remember when you were in elementary school and you found out you would have a substitute teacher the next day? It was a scary moment for most, unless you hated your normal teacher. It was scary because you never knew how strict or vicious the substitute would be, and you would have to be on your best behavior for a few days until you figured them out. Who knew if this substitute was the type to whip out a ruler and smack you across your knuckles, or ferociously dress you down for daring to step out of line?

The next morning, suppose the substitute teacher walks in with impeccable posture and addresses everyone as "mister" and "miss" even though you are eight years old. That's the tone they chose to set, which is obviously not ideal for you. But what if the substitute teacher were to walk in with an untucked shirt and sandals and immediately address the class as "buddies" and "dudes"? I'm not saying one is superior to the other, but a tone is intentionally being set by each of these teachers. It shows you how they prefer to interact with the students, and how they want to be treated.

In conversation and especially when small talk commences, we are sending the same signals, but we probably don't realize it. We are all sizing others up in a similar way, and people are doing the same to you. They look at how you carry yourself, which lets them know what kind of interaction you might prefer. So what kind of substitute teacher do you appear to be to strangers, acquaintances, and even friends?

Knowing you are making an impression on everyone you meet, you should be cognizant of setting the right tone with others. Small talk is of course the verbal portion of the message we are sending out to others, but there are other nonverbal ways to communicate. Maybe small talk wouldn't seem so "small" if we tallied up *all* the data that was really being transmitted in an interaction between two strangers!

What kind of signals are you sending? For our purposes, we ideally want to send a signal of comfort and familiarity. It's understandable that you may not feel comfortable being the first to reach out, but it's too often that this causes a game of chicken where there is no movement at all.

We can keep ourselves from small talk success by talking like strangers, sending signals of discomfort and distance, and simply acting as if we aren't yet friends. When you treat people like strangers, strangers they will remain that way. Setting the tone means making the mental leap to "we're friends now" and treating them as such.

And the best way to do that? In baby steps.

Set the Tone

At the risk of sounding redundant, at the most basic level, this means to speak like friends and stop conversing with everyone like you've just met them at a professional networking event. *How do friends speak, exactly?*

I've got a useful personal anecdote to share on how friends, familiar acquaintances, and those who quickly make friends speak. It was a couple of years ago, and you'll never guess who the other party was.

We had a short back and forth exchanging the normal pleasantries and how-do-you-dos, and then we got right to business. It wasn't particularly what my conversation partner said to me; it was the approach she had. My conversation partner essentially had no filter, and whatever came to her mind, she asked. This was refreshing, as most day-to-day banter can be uniform and vanilla, without a clear path to something more substantive or interesting.

Some people like to shallowly jump from

topic to topic and not truly engage, and this was the opposite experience. The lack of a filter means the conversation will go places that are interesting, emotion-driven, and somewhat inappropriate.

(Of course, the best topics are always somewhat inappropriate. Very few topics are truly inappropriate—you just have to speak about those topics in an appropriate manner.)

Speaking to someone who wasn't beating around the bush for the sake of remaining *appropriate* was refreshing. She wasn't afraid of asking the deep and tough questions, no matter how often she had to ask, "But why?" to understand something. Often, our conversation went down a hole that others would have avoided. She had to ask a few times before I realized myself what I was saying.

There was no judgment, and it was apparent that her questions were motivated by sheer, genuine curiosity. It made me feel comfortable being vulnerable and sharing my more private thoughts. In essence, we had skipped past most phases of small talk and sniffing each other out, and dove right into the deep end and spoke like people who had known each other for a long, long time. Surely this is the type of interaction correlated with general well-being and happiness that was discussed at the opening of this book.

You got me—the conversation partner was an *eight-year-old* I met at an acquaintance's barbecue. For most of us, we have trouble with conversation when we think about it too much. We analyze in our heads, attempt to plan, and unnecessarily filter what we have to say. We stick to conversational rules and get so carried away with our own experience of awkwardness or being appropriate that we forget to see and enjoy the person right in front of us. What comes out when we talk may be "correct" but still overly formal or stilted through overthinking.

No matter how exciting or emotionally engaging the thoughts swimming around our noodles may be, what makes it out of our mouths can be downright dull. So we stick to the tried and proven safe topics. We filter out the excitement and intrigue because we don't want to rile any feathers or because we are self-conscious ourselves. We censor ourselves and make assumptions about what the other person wants to hear from us.

Children do not have this problem, and that's the tone they set. As a result, we all act a certain way toward inquisitive and social children, don't we? We follow their lead. This is always the choice you have as well. Just to be clear, the point is certainly not to act like a child, nor even childlike necessarily. It's just to understand that we all send certain signals when we interact with others, and children send very unique ones that typically open us up and make interactions fun and entertaining.

Within the first few seconds of an interaction, you can set the stage for the kind of engagement that is open, engrossing, novel and genuinely kind. You can treat the interaction as a brand-new, never-before-seen experience, and make your conversation partner feel like they've never been more listened to. Or you can unconsciously send signals that tell the other person, "I'm not *really* interested in this conversation."

Remember not to be so literal and serious; a playful, relaxed attitude like the one you already have with your friends is just right. Be less predictable and give unexpected, unconventional answers. If someone asks how you the traffic was, don't offer a merely descriptive, accurate answer. Make something up, or say the opposite of what you mean (sarcasm in a nutshell). Play with language and use colorful phrases and expressions. Your car is your chariot, the sun is as bright as Elton John's sunglasses, and the orange is as sweet as a truck full of synthetic sugar.

You can bring in some lightheartedness simply by exaggerating a little, being absurd or going over the top in a way that makes people sit up and take notice. When we are a little socially anxious or lacking confidence, we can start to look at conversation as a bit of a battleground—but it's not! It's more like a playground, if you want it to be. At a stressful doctor's appointment, a father may lighten the mood by looking at his pouting toddler with a deadpan expression and saying, "Doctor, is it too late for adoption?"

You may find it effective to deliberately misinterpret a situation in a completely absurd way. If someone says that they love little kids, well, you can fill in the blank there.

Pose hypothetical questions to gently break people out of the regular humdrum of life, or do a silly role play. You're at the library and someone's pencil rolls off the desk and toward you. You catch it and pretend to scold the pencil but then look sadly at the other person. "I'm really sorry, but I don't think your pencil likes you anymore..."

Sarcasm is another tool. An acquaintance asks you how your day at the DMV was and you smile broadly and exclaim, "Fantastic! Have you been? It's just *gorgeous* this time of year stuck inside that luxury hotel."

Sometimes, deliberately drawing attention to the situation you're both in can also create a feeling of camaraderie. When you "break the fourth wall" you talk about exactly what's going on, perhaps having a conversation about the conversation you're having. Many difficult exchanges have actually been revived by someone having the courage to say, "Wow. So this is a little awkward, huh?" If you for some unforeseeable reason happen to spend twenty minutes discussing the merits of chest hair, this would be fair game to point out as a self-referential dig.

What's important here is that none of these things are rules that can be learnt and enforced. Rather, it's an attitude that rests on genuine ease, friendliness and curiosity. This is why people find humor so attractive— those who can laugh at themselves or life are sending a strong message that they are not overwhelmed, stressed or unable to cope. Rather, they are in the mindset of playfulness.

And who doesn't want to have a chat with someone in that mindset?

How do you act like friends otherwise? There is no pretense, there is assumed familiarity, you say what's on your mind, you show your emotions, and you ask deeper questions borne out of curiosity. You don't sit there and worry about if they're judging you, nor do you judge them. There is a feeling of fond comfort, and a sense that you're doing something enjoyable together.

The next time you spend time with a group of friends, try to sit back and analyze the interaction in front of you. Notice the absolute lack of effort. How are people relating to each other, what kind of questions is everyone asking, and what are the signs that you are all comfortable and familiar with each other?

Also pay close attention to the topics being thrown around. You will notice very quickly that they adhere to the small talk stages from the previous chapter. Some facts will be shared, such as stories from people's lives or funny events. Then people will engage in opinion sharing and exchange, and delve even more deeply into how those opinions impact emotions. All of this is done from a perspective of curiosity and genuine interest, rather than with force or a feeling of obligation.

Sometimes it is better to play it safe and be cautious with how we present ourselves. However, those instances do not comprise the majority of our lives. The biggest lesson from this section should be that we are indeed capable of setting the tone, and most of us do it in a way that is self-defeating—but we are capable of changing that if we put in a little effort.

Make the First Move

We're ready to start chatting. Of course, I'm talking about breaking the ice. For most of us, this is what we imagine when we are trying to create an initial impression.

To be frank, it's not that we don't know what to say—just like with when we forget someone's name, we know the most direct path to getting what we want. We should just ask. And so the easiest and most direct way of breaking the ice is to just say hello and introduce your name. But this isn't helpful for most of us because we typically feel too uncomfortable to be so direct. Thus arises the need for sly tactics to accomplish what we want through indirect means.

The whole world of dating "pickup" tactics, and the idea that you need to have some sort of game or move or strategy to approach other people, reinforces this disastrous idea. We seem to forget how we'd behave in the other position: most people would say that if they were casually approached with genuine interest and respectful friendliness, they would respond positively. Yet somehow, we feel too uncomfortable taking the first step ourselves.

Our discomfort happens for a multitude of reasons, summed up by the feeling that we are interrupting people or otherwise inconveniencing them. We have trouble breaking the ice with strangers, even though it's such a simple thing, because we create a "they'll think" or "what if" feedback loop in our brains.

What can I say to avoid being awkward? What if I'm interrupting them? Will they think I'm stupid? What if they are busy? What should I say? What can I say?

For instance, if we chat up a stranger or barge into two people already having a conversation, we are afraid:

- They'll think I'm a weirdo.
- They'll think I'm a creep.
- They'll think I'm rude.
- They'll be annoyed.
- What if they want to speak in private?
- What if they hate my face already?

It doesn't matter that these aren't true—we *think* they are true, so they block us from easy solutions to the problem of breaking the ice. In the matter of making introductions, we need to find tactics to undercut the judgments and assumptions we make of ourselves. The (maybe boring?) truth is that most people are rather indifferent to other people making the first move. It's only anxiety and our own biases that make us assume a negative response where there in fact is nothing worse than a neutral one.

So how can you feel okay about breaking the ice? By doing it indirectly. In other words, having some sort of excuse or justification to speak to someone—when we have come up with a reason, suddenly it's easy to interrupt people or walk up to a stranger.

For instance, suppose that you are intensely shy and nervous. You eschew most forms of social interaction. But if you were utterly lost and on the verge of exhaustion, would you have a problem walking up to someone and asking for directions? Doubtful, and not just because of necessity. You'd feel that you have a compelling reason to speak, and that would override your fear of judgment.

That's the meaning of indirect in this context: you have an actual reason to approach someone, and when we can create one for ourselves, we can convince ourselves to take action more easily. In other instances, you might refer to this as the feeling of *plausible deniability*—where you have a plausible reason to walk up and start a conversation in a way that no one can think you're rude or weird. *Actually, if they think you're rude or weird, they're the rude or weird ones.*

But again, this is a trick we use to get around our own discomfort and anxiety, and not the negative response of others. If we can convince *ourselves* that we have a legitimate reason for intruding on another person's space or conversation, then we feel more able to do it. Think of it like confidence training wheels. When you've become surer in your social abilities, you may not need a pretense anymore, and won't feel embarrassed to just talk directly to people.

In the meantime, I want to present three indirect methods of breaking the ice that help you feel safe because you aren't necessarily walking up to someone just for the sake of starting a conversation. The biggest part of the battle is making breaking the ice feel acceptable—it's an "I don't feel confident or comfortable" issue more than an "I don't know what to say" issue. Recall that asking for directions on the verge of exhaustion makes all of those worries secondary.

The first, indirect method of breaking the ice is to ask people for *objective information* or a *subjective opinion*. These can be very legitimate and important questions that would necessitate speaking to a stranger. It doesn't necessarily matter that the person you are asking knows the answer; it's just a way to begin a dialogue. For that matter, it doesn't even matter that you *don't* know the answer.

- Excuse me, do you know what time the speeches begin?
- Do you know where the closest Starbucks is?
- What did you think of the CEO's speech?
- Do you like the food here?

The first two examples are inquiring about

objective information, while the latter two are asking for a subjective opinion.

The second, indirect method of breaking the ice is to comment on something in the environment, context, or specific situation. It can be as simple as an observation. Imagine you are thinking out loud and prompting people to answer.

- Did you see that piece of art on the wall? What a crazy concept.
- The lighting in here is beautiful. I think it's worth more than my house.
- This is an amazing DJ. All the rock ballads of the '80s.

Notice how these are all statements and not direct questions. You are inviting someone to comment on your statement instead of asking them to engage. If they don't choose to engage, no harm no foul. You are not putting any pressure on them to respond, and you don't necessarily need to expect an answer.

The third and final indirect method of breaking the ice is to comment on a commonality you both share. For instance, why are you both at your friend Jack's apartment? What business brings you both to this networking conference in Tallahassee?

What stroke of misfortune brought you to the DMV this morning?

- So who do you know here?
- So how do you know Jack?
- Has Jack told you about the time he went skiing with his dog?

The idea with these commonalities is that they are instant topics of conversation because there will be a clear answer behind them. These indirect icebreakers aren't rocket science, but their main value is to make you feel okay with engaging someone in conversation, which is the real problem.

You don't need any particular skills or confidence to pull these off. In fact, if the person you're speaking to is perceptive enough, they can probably tell that you're using a pretense to open a dialogue. In any case, most people will respond positively to someone making the effort to do that, so there really isn't much to lose. Don't worry about rehearsing too much or finding the right words. The idea is just to make that first step. Eventually you may get to the point where you feel comfortable just walking up to someone and shaking their hand, but in the meantime, you can get started here.

Find Similarity

Think back to the last time you met someone new at a networking event or party. What was the first topic out of your mouth? It was probably one of the following:

- Where are you from?
- Who do you know here?
- How was your weekend?
- Where did you go to school?
- What do you do?
- Do you live far from here?

While these are normal small-talk questions, we ask them instinctively not because they are great at breaking the ice. In fact, as you well know, they are usually terrible for breaking the ice and can make people feel immediately bored. You may have had a negative physical reaction at reading those prompts.

We actually ask these questions instinctively because we are searching for commonalities. We are searching for the "me too!" moment that can spark a deeper discussion, and thus improve the first impression. For instance, if we ask the question "Where did you go to school?" we are hoping they attended the same university as us or a university where we have mutual friends. The next natural question is a variation of "Oh wow! What a small world. Do you know James Taylor? He also went there around your time."

While you may not realize it, you are always hunting for similarities, and similarities are another way of setting a tone of friendship, familiarity, comfort, and openness. It's the type of feeling you share with your friends, and the same feeling that can instantly skyrocket your rapport.

As much as we would like to think that we are open-minded and can get along with people from every background and origin, the reality is that we usually get along best with people who we think are like us. In fact, we seek them out.

This trait is why places like Little Italy, Chinatown, and Koreatown exist. But I'm not just talking about race, skin color, religion, or sexual orientation. I'm talking about people who share our values, look at the world the same way we do, and have the same take on things as we do. As the saying goes, birds of a feather flock together. This is a common human tendency that is rooted in how our species developed. Walking out on the tundra or in a forest, you would be conditioned to avoid that which is unfamiliar or foreign because there is a high likelihood it would be interested in killing you.

Similarities make us relate better to other people because we think they'll understand us on a deeper level. If we share at least one significant similarity, then all sorts of positive traits follow, because we see them as our contemporary, essentially an extension of ourselves. When you think someone is on your level, you want to connect with them because they will probably understand you better than most.

Suppose you were born in a small village in South Africa. The population of the village ranges from 900 to 1000 people. You now live in London and you are attending a party at a friend's home. You meet someone that also happens to be from that small village in South Africa, just eight years older so you never encountered each other.

What warm feelings will you immediately have toward this other person, and what assumptions will you make about them? How interested will you be in connecting with them and spending more time together in the future? What inside jokes or specialized points of reference can you discuss that you haven't been able to with anyone else, ever?

Hopefully that illustration drives home the value of similarity and how it drives conversational connection. So as mentioned, we typically use small-talk questions to find similarity, but there are better, more effective ways to discover commonalities with people. For instance, we should always be *searching* for similarities or *creating* opportunities for them. They both take effort and initiative. Let's talk about searching for similarities first.

We can *search* for similarities by asking probing questions of people and using their answers as the basis to show connections, no matter how small. Ask questions to figure out what people are about, what they like, and how they think. Then dig deep into yourself to find small commonalities at first, such as favorite baseball teams or alcoholic drinks. Through those smaller commonalities, you'll be able to figure out what makes them tick and find deeper similarities to instantly bond over. Just as you'd be thrilled to meet someone from that small South African town, you'd be ecstatic to meet someone who shared a love of the same obscure hobby as you.

It doesn't take months or years, and it doesn't take a special circumstance like going through military boot camp together. It just requires you to look outside of yourself and realize that people share common attitudes, experiences, and emotions—you just have to find them. Get comfortable asking questions and digging deeper than you naturally would. (Is it odd for you to ask five questions in a row? It shouldn't be.) It might even feel a little invasive at first. Find the shared experiences and use them.

For each topic, you can find some part to relate to and connect on, instead of digging around a variety of shallow topics like a job interview. Don't stop at the initial topic—if someone says they love baseball, for instance, you could try to understand why that is and what makes them such a fanatic for a game involving hitting a ball with an oversized stick. Suppose their love for baseball came from their father, to whom they are particularly close—well, you have (or had) a father at some point, also with a relationship (hopefully good). That's quite a powerful similarity. Searching for similarities will come more easily in most cases.

Naturally, you need to be careful that, when you're seeking out similarities, you don't accidentally alienate the other person or put them on the spot. Take a look at this (sadly all too common) exchange:

A: "Hey, have you seen XYZ series?"
B: "Uh, no, I've heard it's popular, but I haven't seen it myself!"
A: "Oh. You should totally watch it, though. It's great. It's a lot like [names very similar series]. Have you seen that?"
B: "Hm, no, doesn't ring a bell."
A: "No?! Oh you're missing out. What about [gives yet another related show]? Please tell me you've seen that, right?"

You can see the problem. Rather than A's questions helping to find any point of commonality and encourage those warm-fuzzies, they're doing the opposite, and making B feel like they're out of the loop, uninformed, or just have bad taste. It's worth remembering that commonality goes beyond just liking the same music or being familiar with the same cultural references.. Look at another way this conversation could have gone:

A: "Hey, have you seen XYZ series?"
B: "Uh, no, I've heard it's popular, but I haven't seen it myself!"
A: "Oh, it's great. One of those Scandinavian

cop drama things... Depends how moody you like your main characters to be!"
B: *"Ah, moody? No thanks, there's enough drama for me in real life..."*
A: *"Yeah? So you're a comedy person then?"*
B: *"Well, it's funny you ask..." [and so on].*

In this second dialogue, A swiftly moves on to another potential area of commonality, and asks indirectly what B likes in TV series. It doesn't feel like a put-you-on-the-spot interview anymore, but rather like a genuinely friendly and curious conversation between two people.

In addition to searching out what is already there, we can *create* opportunities for similarities in a few ways—first physically by mimicking people's body language, voice tonality, rate of speech, and overall manner of appearance. This is known as *mirroring*, and it has also been shown to produce feelings of positivity when tested (Anderson, 1998). All you have to do is arrange yourself to resemble others in order to benefit from feelings of similarity, from how they are posed to how they gesture.

You can mirror their words, their tone of voice, and their mannerisms. Keep in mind that mirroring is not just about reflecting the person on a wholesale basis. Instead, it is all about communicating to them that you share similar values and have the potential to connect intimately. The great thing about this approach is that it happens in real time, right there in the moment. The conversation itself becomes a shared experience.

You can mirror physical signals, gestures, tics, and mannerisms. For example, if you notice that someone uses a lot of gestures when talking, you should do the same. Similarly, if you notice that someone's body language involves a lot of leaning and crossing of arms, you should follow their lead. You can mirror their verbal expressions and expressiveness—tone of voice, inflection, word choice, slang and vocabulary, emotional intonation, and excitement and energy. This has the overall effect of making people feel more heard, feel more subconsciously comfortable and familiar with you, and fostering feelings of closeness relatively quickly.

The second way to create opportunities for similarities is to ensure that you share a healthy amount of personal information and divulge details—probably more than what you are used to.

What did you do last month?

Statement one: *You went skiing last month.*
Statement two: *You went skiing last month with your two brothers and you almost broke your foot. Thank goodness you have a background in dance so you were able to keep yourself from serious injury.*

Which of those stories is easier to relate to and find a similarity with? Obviously, the second version since there is literally four times as much information. If you are having trouble connecting with others, it's likely you are expecting to find a similarity without sharing anything yourself. Let's do another one.

How does your week look?

Statement one: *This week seems pretty busy.*
Statement two: *Pretty busy, my mother-in-law is coming into town so that should be "fun." I think I also need to find a cobbler and an ice-cream cake for a party I'm going to.*

If sharing even this amount of detail feels uncomfortable and unnatural for you, it's a sign you probably don't give your conversation partners much to work with, and you are essentially dropping the conversational ball when it is hit back to you. You may be the cause of awkward silence more often than not, because others will expect a back and forth flow, but they end up doing all the work while you wonder what's wrong. In other words, get used to this feeling of discomfort because it's something you need to improve upon.

Aside from searching for similarities and creating opportunities for them, consider that *mutual dislike* is a useful bonding agent. Have you noticed that it is sometimes impossible for the conversation to remain positive, and the conversation will veer into a set of complaints about something you both dislike? Simply put, mutual *dislike* creates a sense of excitement that can often be more powerful than mutual *like*.

For instance, discovering that you both went to the same restaurant, were served by the same waiter, and both hated him. It's easy to discount these interactions because people think talking about negativity is a negative thing. However, it's not negative to talk about negativity because it's an emotion like any other, and the more emotion you can generate in your interaction, the greater an impression you will make.

What's ultimately important is seeing eye-to-eye in some fashion, preferably one that is about your opinions, views, emotions, or choices/decisions. They can be positive or negative—the goal is just to converge on something.

Manufacture Connection

Sometimes, despite all the groundwork you've put into setting a friendly tone, making the first move, and even digging out some underrated similarities, people won't engage too much. Some people just aren't very forthcoming. Conversing with them can be like talking to walls for no apparent reason. You can ask them something seemingly innocent, and they just dodge, demur, or give you a one-word answer. Whatever the case, conversation has now come to a full stop.

Unfortunately, they have set the tone to treat you as a stranger and hold you at arm's length, which is something we are making sure we don't do ourselves. The reasons for this can vary, but most of them are not related to you. Moreover, often we cannot control this. But that's okay, there are ways to move past this type of engagement (if you are certain that they are actually interested in engaging with you, versus stonewalling you in the hopes that you leave them alone). In a sense, this is you manufacturing a connection out of nothing at all—at least, whatever your conversation/small talk partner is giving you.

This is where the practice of *elicitation* comes in. It is a type of questioning that uses a specific conversational style to encourage people to share and speak more. It was originally developed by the Federal Bureau of Investigation (FBI) for use during interrogations, but was quickly adopted by corporate spies to obtain confidential information from competitors.

Its origins will probably give you pause, but all of these techniques can be used for both good and evil. The methods themselves are neutral and are a result of taking a look into the human psyche.

To use elicitation, you make a statement that plays on the other person's desire to respond for a variety of reasons. The other person will feel driven to respond, even if they had no prior interest in engaging. They will almost feel like they have no choice. A direct question will not always get an answer; thus, it becomes important to ask indirect questions to encourage opening up and creating engagement.

Here is an example of how elicitation works. You are trying to plan a surprise party for someone, so you need to know his schedule, his friends' contact information, and his food and drink preferences. Of course, you can't ask him for this information directly. So how might you indirectly obtain this information from him? Ellen Naylor, in her 2016 book *Win/Loss Analysis,* wrote about a few elicitation techniques to get people talking.

Recognition. People thrive when you recognize something good about them. Mention "I love your sweater" and you will get a story about how the wearer obtained the sweater. Mention "You are very thorough" and you will get a story about how the person went to military school and learned to be thorough at all times. They may have been tight-lipped before, but any chance to enhance praise is welcome. People have a natural desire to feel recognized and appreciated, so give them an opening to show off a little.

You can also show appreciation to someone and compliment them. This is similar to recognition; people rarely turn down an opportunity to explain their accomplishments.

Complaining. We've covered this a bit in talking about how people love mutual dislike. People also love to complain, so it is easy to get someone to open up by giving them something to commiserate with. You complain first, and they will jump at the opportunity. If they don't join in, they might open up the other way by feeling compelled to defend what you are complaining about. Either way, you've opened them up.

You might tell someone at work, "I hate these long hours without overtime pay," and he will agree and go into more detail about how he needs money from not being paid enough. This may lead him to disclose more about his home life and how many kids he has and marital issues he has related to finances. It may also lead him to defend the long hours. Either way, you have more information now.

Key to this technique is creating a safe environment for people to brag, complain, or show other raw emotion. If you complain first, you establish a judgment-free zone. They don't feel like they will get in trouble with you. You don't have to complain to kickstart this; just express your own negative emotions, vulnerabilities, or disappointments.

Correction. People love to be right. This is truly the backbone of any Internet argument. So if you say something wrong, they will gladly jump at the chance to correct you. If you give people an opportunity to flex their ego, most will seize it happily.

An easy way to do this is to state something you know to be obviously incorrect to see if they will step in and break their silence. See if they can resist this primal urge.

Naïveté. To be clear, this does not mean to act stupid; it means to act like you're on the *cusp* of understanding. Acting naïve makes people feel compelled to teach, instruct, and show off their knowledge. People just can't resist enlightening you, especially if you're 95 percent of the way there and all people have to do is figuratively finish your sentence. "I understand most of this theory, but there's just this one thing I'm unclear on. It could mean so many things…" People won't be able to stop themselves from jumping in.

In the spirit of elicitation, here are a few indirect methods that I've discovered work quite well for me personally.

When you ask a question you think may not be answered, act as if they answered it and react to that hypothetical answer.

You: So I hear that project didn't go so well at work?
Bob: Yeah. Not great.
You: Yeah, I heard things were going excellent minus that little snafu at the end of the quarter. But that's no one's fault. That part of the project is super complex. It's crazy. I can't believe it even got the green light.

When you put all of this on the table, it's going to be nearly irresistible for them to step in and answer, reply, correct, confirm, or deny. That's the important part—you are (1) asking a question, (2) acting as if *they* answered the question, and (3) then seeing how they react to your assumption of their answer. Don't wait for them to react to your question; just give them the opportunity to react to your subsequent answer. The premise here is that even if they don't want to talk to you, they'll be forced to engage and step in to intervene in some way. You may not get the merriest of answers, but the important thing is that you've gotten them to open their traps in the first place, and that can be the hardest part of all.

There's another variation on this method of getting people to engage or otherwise speak up. *When you ask someone a question, assume they are going to answer a certain way and keep elaborating on that sentiment.* Again, if you're lucky, people will feel compelled to correct you and clarify what their actual answer to the question is.

You: So how was the vacation? I bet it was terrible with all of those worms and alligators. I hate the water and humidity so much.
Bobby: Well, actually...

Gotcha! In the same vein, you can elicit people to speak and open up more by talking about something you know is obviously wrong and waiting for them to jump in.

You: That relationship seemed so good because he has a nice car, right? That's all you need. I guess when it's a Corvette it's enough. Money is life.
Bobby: Well, actually...

These methods capitalize on people's instinct to set the record straight. Even if they don't want to talk about something, they don't want the incorrect or negative perception floating around about them. If you were only getting one word out of them, and you are able to eke two sentences out of them by using this tactic, consider it a win to keep building on.

Remember that the tone of an exchange is something you have 100 percent ability to set. Many of us feel that conversations are a matter of luck—you strike it lucky by finding a mutual topic of interest or similarity, and those instances are necessary to create rapport. Of course, if you believe this to be the case, it *will* be the case for you.

Takeaways:

- What determines whether you hit it off with someone? It's not circumstantial; rather, it's a matter of you taking charge and setting the tone to be friendly and open. Most people treat others like strangers and thus won't become friends. So change that script from the very beginning, put people at ease and let them be comfortable around you.
- The first way to set the tone is to speak like friends: topic-wise, tone-wise, and even privacy-wise. People will go along with the tone you set as long as you aren't outright offensive. A powerful aspect of this is showing emotion as friends do, instead of filtering yourself and putting up a wall for the literal purpose of keeping

people insulated at a distance. And stop being so darned literal and serious. A conversation does not have to be about sharing facts, and some comments can be used solely for the purpose of seeing how the other person will react.

- Another aspect of setting the right tone is to search for similarities and also allow the opportunity to create them. When people observe similarity, they instantly open up and embrace it because it is a reflection of themselves. There are only good assumptions and connotations, so we should actively seek them out. You can do this by digging more deeply into people's lives and asking questions to find seemingly unrelated similarities, divulging more information yourself, and also mirroring them physically. Also, don't discount the value of *mutual dislike*—it's not negative to talk about negative things, per se.

- Finally, even if you follow these steps, sometimes people either aren't willing to engage or not good at opening up themselves. You can blast past this by using forms of *elicitation*, in which you put forth a topic or question in a way that a person will feel compelled to engage or elaborate. These take the form of prompting the person to reply to your recognition, encouraging mutual complaining, assisting your naiveté, and correcting your incorrect assumption or information.

Chapter 3. How to be Captivating

Captivating is a pretty strong word, and as such, it's probably something that we want to strive for in our interactions.

When we think of a captivating person, what kind of mental image comes to mind? If you were to choose a picture for a "captivating person" in a dictionary, what would the person be? What is this person expressing, how are they acting, and what are you watching them do?

More often than not, this person is going to look like they are on a stage or pulpit gesticulating grandly and expressively, with an emotion-filled face. And I would also bet that this person is in the middle of weaving an engrossing tale that captivates his or her audience. Indeed, if you think about it, it seems that only with storytelling can we mesmerize and charm others into hanging on to our every word.

Okay, that's up for debate, but determining whether or not that is true is not the aim of this chapter. No one can deny that storytelling is an important element of memorable conversations and discussions that you want to have. The question is always how to capture this elusive skill and make it your own. Therefore, in this chapter, I want to present a few perspectives on how you can use storytelling in your everyday conversations and even small talk.

It's helpful to first take the mystique away from the whole concept of storytelling. What is storytelling? It's just telling someone about something that happened. That's all. Of course, there are better and worse ways to do this, but at the core, storytelling is just talking about the past in a way that makes people pay attention. The first part we have no problem with—we've all described our pasts, and we all have great experiences worthy of being told—but the second part is typically the challenge. With that in mind, let's see how we can get better at storytelling.

A Life of Stories

To get better at stories, we have to begin to recognize them in our daily lives. No, seriously. We don't think of our lives as being very interesting on a day-to-day basis, but we do quite a bit more than we realize. It's not that every day you are engaging in a massive protest that you can tell your kids about, or you were chased by a wiener dog down a dark alley whereupon a man dressed as a parrot saved you by tackling the dog. These stories are self-evident and don't need any organization or special way of telling them to make an impact.

People who naturally have the "gift of the gab" may be known for adding a little artistic flare (or outright embellishment!) to their stories, but that's because they have an instinctual understanding of the fact that almost anything, when told in the right way, can be a great story. If you've ever seen a legendary storyteller weave a humorous "shaggy dog" tale about nothing more than that misunderstanding they had at the post office yesterday, you'll know that style is way more important than content.

We have to draw from our daily lives, and believe me, there is plenty to draw from. Your life is far more interesting than you know, believe me! It's just a matter of seeing the mini-stories that are inherent in our everyday existence. What is the definition of a mini-story in this context?

"So what do you do?"
"I'm a marketing executive."

Well, not that. That's going to get a reply of "Oh, cool. I'm going to the bathroom now, goodbye." Let's try again.

"So what do you do?"
"I'm a marketing executive. I deal mostly with clients. Just last week we had a crazy client that threatened to send his bodyguards to our office! I definitely wish I dealt more with the creative side."

There we go. This will probably garner a stronger response than wanting to escape to the bathroom, such as "Oh my God! Did he actually send them? TELL ME MORE."

That's a mini-story. It's answering questions (or spontaneously sharing) briefly using the elements of a story—an action that occurs to a subject with some sort of conclusion. As you can see above, a brief mini-story will create exponentially more conversation and interest than any answer to the question, "What do you do?" All you needed was three sentences. Try reading it out loud—it takes less than ten seconds, and you've jam-packed it with enough information to be interesting to anyone.

What's great about mini-stories is you can also create these before a conversation, so you can have compelling anecdotes at hand in response to very common and widespread questions. The main benefit to creating mini-stories ahead of time is to be able to avoid one-word answers that you may be accustomed to using. This can give a sense of confidence going in, because you've prepared for what will come.

When you break down the context surrounding a mini-story, they become much simpler. Shoot for three sentences that can answer some of the most common conversation topics that will arise.

1. Your occupation (if you have a job that is unusual or nebulous, make sure you have a layman's description of your job that people can relate to)
2. Your week
3. Your upcoming weekend
4. Your hometown

5. Your hobbies and so on.

When you are using a mini-story to answer a question, make sure to first acknowledge the question that was asked. But then, realizing that you have something far more interesting to say, you can jump into the mini-story, which should be able to stand by itself.

"How was your weekend?"
"It was fine. I watched four *Star Wars* movies."
"Okay, I'm going to go talk to someone else now."

Let's try again.

"How was your weekend?"
"It was fine, but did I tell you about what happened last Friday? A dog wearing a tuxedo walked into my office and he peed on everything."
"Wait. Tell me more."

Using mini-stories allows you to avoid the tired back of forth of "Good, how about you" you'll find in everyday small talk. That's the first step to being captivating.

It might help to reframe mini-stories this way: when people make small talk with you and ask any of the classic small-talk questions, they aren't truly interested in the answers to those questions. They want to hear something interesting, so give it to them.

This is an important point to repeat: when we ask how someone's weekend was, or what people's travel plans are, we usually aren't that interested in the literal answer. We've already talked about how you should disclose and divulge more about yourself in an effort to find more similarities, and now you can see another benefit of offering more.

Not only that, mini-stories are an inside view to the way you think and feel. They give clues to your mindset, personality, and emotional leanings. Learning about those aspects is the first step in allowing anyone to relate and feel connected to you, so it's imperative that you learn how to take any question and expand it to your advantage. It will also encourage them to reciprocate.

Think about what most compels you to pay attention to any story or anecdote. Usually, a good story has some relatable human element to it, some sense of direction or conflict, or the topic being described is universally appealing and interesting to people. For example, almost everyone loves cute pets, juicy gossip, happy endings, funny and embarrassing moments, or unexpected twists. On the other hand, only a few people are going to pay attention to a story about international banking regulations ad how they slightly changed in Switzerland last Thursday.

Mini-stories also underscore the importance of providing more details, as mentioned in an earlier chapter, and avoiding one-word answers. Details offer a three-dimensional description of you and your life. That automatically makes people more interested and invested because they are already painting a mental picture in their minds and visualizing everything.

Details also give people more to connect to, think about, and attach themselves to. With more details, there is a substantially higher likelihood that people will find something funny, interesting, in common, poignant, curious, and worthy of comment in what you have to say.

Detail and specificity put people into a particular place and time. This allows them to imagine exactly what's happening and start caring about it. Think about why it's so easy to get sucked into a movie. We experience enormous sensory stimulation and almost can't escape all of the visual and auditory detail, which is designed to make us invested. Detailed stories and conversations are inviting others to share a mental movie with you.

Beyond giving flavor to your conversation and storytelling, and giving the other person something to ask about, details are important because they elicit emotional engagement. Details remind people of their own lives and memories and make them feel more drawn to whatever is presenting them. Details can compel others to laugh, feel mad, feel sad, or feel surprise. They can control moods and emotions.

If you include details about specific songs that played during your high school dances, it's likely that someone will have memories attached to those songs and become more emotionally interested in your story. Use all the five senses to describe everything that went wrong on that hilarious blind date you had. Share details about all the figurative nooks and crannies, because that's what makes you interesting on an emotional level. Paint a picture for your listeners, and draw them into that world.

The 1:1:1 Method

On the theme of simplifying storytelling, we've been talking about how we can use a mini-story in many ways. You may be wondering what the difference is between a *mini* story and a *full-fledged* story.

For our purposes, not much. It seems that many people like to complicate storytelling as if they were composing an impromptu Greek tragedy. Does there have to be an introduction, middle, struggle, then resolution? Does there need to be a hero, a conflict, and an emotional journey? Not necessarily. Those are specific ways of storytelling if you are Francis Ford Coppola (director of the *Godfather* series) or a standup comedian used to keeping crowds engaged.

But certainly these aren't the easiest or most practical ways to think about storytelling.

My method of storytelling in conversation is to prioritize the discussion afterward. This means that the story itself doesn't need to be that in-depth or long. It can and should contain specific details that people can relate to and latch on to, but it doesn't need to have parts or stages. A full story can be *mini* by nature. That's why it's called the *1:1:1 method.*

This method stands for a story that (1) has one action, (2) can be summed up in one sentence, and (3) evokes one primary emotion in the listener. You can see why they're short and snappy. They also tend to ensure that you know your point before starting and have a very low chance of verbally wandering for minutes and alienating your listeners. This is the lowest input to the highest output ratio you can have for a story.

Let's look at how to construct these simple-as-possible mini stories. For a story to consist of *one action* means only one thing is happening. The story is about one occurrence, one event. It should be direct and straightforward. Anything else just confuses the point and makes you liable to ramble. Details are important to share, but probably not at the outset because the story's impact will be lost or blunted.

A story should be able to be *summed up* in one sentence because, otherwise, you are trying to convey too much. And if you're an anxious person, a longer story might just give you more opportunities to worry about your delivery (you know that sinking feeling of forgetting how a joke goes midway through telling it?).

Sticking to one single action keeps you focused and straight to the point. This step actually takes practice, because you are forced to think about which aspects of the story matter and which don't add anything to your action. Imagine you are creating the verbal equivalent of a single-panel cartoon, where the setup and punchline are all in one place. It's a skill to be able to distill your thoughts into one sentence and still be thorough—often, you won't realize what you want to say unless you can do this.

Finally, a story should focus on one primary emotion to be evoked in the listener. And you should be able to name it! Keep in mind that evoking an emotion ensures that your story actually has a point, and it will color what details you carefully choose to emphasize that emotion. For our purposes here, there really aren't that many emotions you might want to draw out in others from a story. You might have humor, shock, awe, envy, happiness, anger, or annoyance. Those are the majority of reasons we relate our experiences to others.

Keep in mind that this is just my method for

conveying my experiences to others. My logic is that whether people hear two sentences about a dog attack or they hear ten sentences doesn't change the impact of the story. Telling a story about your friend going to jail—well, he's still in jail at the end of two or ten sentences. Likewise, if you tell a story about how you adopted a dog, the dog will still be lounging on your bed if you take ten seconds or two minutes to tell the story.

A bad storyteller might dwell on a longer, more convoluted tale that actually bores everyone because they fundamentally misunderstand the point of storytelling in the first place. Remember that even though you are trying to tell a compelling story, you are not really an entertainer on a stage. Your primary goal is not to get people to applaud and think you're awesome—the goal is to make other people feel relaxed and happy, and to get good, satisfying conversation flowing. And that means, the sooner you can get off your podium, the better!

After you provide the premise, the conversation can move forward as a dialogue, your conversation partner can participate more fully, and we can then focus on the listener's impact and reaction. Then you can let the inevitable questions flow, and you can slowly divulge the details after the context is set, and the initial impact is felt. So what does this so-called story sound like?

"I was attacked by a dog and I was so frightened I nearly wet my pants." It's one sentence, there is one action, and the bit about wetting the pants is to emphasize the fact that the emotion you want to convey is fear and shock.

You could include more detail about the dog and the circumstances, but chances are people are going to ask about that immediately, so let them guide what they want to hear about your story. It doesn't hurt to directly name the emotion that you were experiencing. Invite them to participate! Very few people want to sit and listen to a monologue, most of which is told poorly and in a scattered manner.

Therefore, keep the essentials but cut your story short, and let the conversation continue as a shared experience rather than you monopolizing the airspace. Think about it. Which is more engrossing and interesting: having your listeners prompt you to please tell them more, because they're on the edge of their seat, or you reciting a boring stand-up routine where your audience is not really required to do much but listen? Here are another couple of easy examples:

"*Last week, I had a job interview that went so poorly I had the interviewer laugh at me while I was leaving the office, it was so embarrassing.*" One action, one emotion, in one sentence.

"*When I first met Joshua, I spilled a bowl of baked beans all over his white pants and I think the entire room was watching while this happened.*"

The 1:1:1 method can be summed up as starting a story as close to the end as possible. Most stories end before they get to the end, in terms of impact on the listener, their attention span, and the energy that you have to tell it. In other words, many stories tend to drone on because people try to adhere to complex rules or because they simply lose the plot and are trying to find it again through talking. Above all else, a long preamble is not necessary. What's important is that people pay attention, care, and will react in some (preferably) emotional manner.

The Story Spine

Think of the story spine as an upgraded and

expanded version of the 1:1:1 method. It gives you the beats of a great story in a simple formula.

This technique can be credited to Kevin Adams, author and the artistic director of Synergy Theater. He teaches how the "story spine" can be used to outline a great story. This method is perfect for novelists and film makers, but you can also use it whenever you want to entertain friends with a tale that will have them riveted. Likewise, it can tell you why certain stories completely fall flat, since it shows you what crucial elements may be missing.

It can be done quickly and, with practice, may start feeling automatic. If you're feeling confident using the 1:1:1 method, you might like to try the story spine approach and see what happens.

The story spine has eight elements; here's how they go:

Once upon a time...

The start of the story. Here, you must set the context and lay out the world you're talking about and the characters you'll be focusing on. You establish their routine, normal reality. If you skip this part your story may seem inconsequential, or people won't be able to make sense of the events that follow and why they matter.

Every day...

More establishing of the normal and routine. Often, a character is growing bored, sad or curious, and this drives the next stages of the story. This step builds tension, and is the place you give your characters a personality and a motive for what happens next. You don't want to spend too much time here, however—your listeners need to get the sense that you are just setting the stage, because something unusual and exciting is about to happen.

But one day...

And here comes the big event that changes everything! One day, something different happens that completely turns your character's world around. A stranger comes to town or a mysterious clue shows up. What normally happens didn't happen today. Here, really dig into the *emotion* attached to the big change that's come along.

Because of that...

There are consequences. The main character acts in response, and this sets into motion the main body of the story, the "what happened" part. Now we have a moving, dynamic narrative. Many poor storytellers will simply leap in and begin here, failing to build tension or set any context, and then discover that their audience isn't as invested in the outcome. Like good conversation skills, good storytelling skills require pacing and *gradual* building of tension.

Because of that...

Things get more interesting or frightening, the stakes are raised, the plot thickens, other characters enter and a whole world of complications/comedy/drama opens up as the story plays out. Here, you want to increase the emotional response. The details are important, but they're there to drive home the emotional stakes and impact of what's happening.

Because of that...

Good stories appeal to our love for the number three in our narratives. That's why we have Goldilocks and the three bears, and why the hero typically faces three challenges before finally making it. Take the time to really explore the three dilemmas the character faces, and you make the resolution that much sweeter.

Until finally...

Does the guy get the girl? Was the world saved or did the detective find out who did it? Here's where you reveal all. The conflict is resolved, and the story is wrapped up. If your story is well-constructed, your audience has likely been listening all the way because they're waiting for this big reveal, this final outcome. So, they'd better not be disappointed!

And ever since then...

You close the story as you began it—with some context. You outline here what the new normal is, given the character's success or failure at the previous step. You could consider a moral of the story here, or a little joke or punchline. In conversation, this tells people you're done with your story and signals them to respond.

What's important to remember about a story spine is that it's just that—a spine. You still need to add considerable flesh to the outline to make it compelling. The story spine merely makes sure you're hitting the right notes in the right order, and gives you a satisfying structure to follow.

Not every story will follow it exactly (it's only a rough outline, after all) but if yours do, there's a good chance they'll be better received than narratives that are a bit more experimental. Some narratives work precisely because they violate our expectations of what stories should do, but this is typically a harder thing to get right, and can flop more easily than a tried-and-true tale.

As an example, consider the popular theme song for the '80s TV show *The Fresh Prince of Bel-Air*. This shows that even in a quick story, it's important to have the essential building blocks. The song starts:

In west Philadelphia born and raised
On the playground is where I spent most of my days
Chillin' out maxin' relaxin' all cool
And all shootin' some b-ball outside of the school

This covers "once upon a time" and "every day." Context established.

When a couple of guys who were up to no good
Started makin' trouble in my neighborhood
I got in one little fight and my mom scared
And said you're movin' with your auntie and
uncle in Bel-Air

Here's the "but one day" part that changes
everything.

I begged and pleaded with her day after day
But she packed my suitcase and sent me on my
way... etc.

The middle portion of the song covers him
begging with his mom not to go, getting on a
plane to Bel-Air and then taking a cab, while
slowly grasping the whole new world he's
just walked into. This is the middle of the
story, the three "and because of that"
portions. The final verse goes:

I pulled up to the house about 7 or 8
And I yelled to the cabbie yo homes smell ya
later
Looked at my kingdom I was finally there
To sit on my throne as the prince of Bel-Air

"And finally" and "since then" are rolled into
one here, and the new normal is established,
with the main character happily set up in his

new life. Granted, there isn't too much conflict or tension here, but the structure is sound.

Consider someone using the story spine in a more everyday context: a dispute at work. Someone is trying to explain what's happened clearly to an external mediator. Their story sounds like this:

"Melissa and Jake both work in the IT department, they run things together with Barbara, who's now on maternity leave. Melissa's been with the company for more than ten years, and Jake is new, so Melissa has been informally training him to cover Barbara's work for the next six months, possibly longer term (there are rumors Jake will get Barbara's job if she leaves). They've been working on a big project together for the last month.

"Unknown to us, Melissa and Jake had a brief relationship months back that ended badly.

"Because of that there's been some tension in the office. There was a crucial mistake on the big project and Melissa was held accountable. But she's since revealed to us that it was in fact Jake's fault, and she had covered for him while they were still in a relationship.

Because of this, Jake is claiming that Melissa is only blaming him now because they are no longer in a relationship, which he believes is unfair.

"Eventually, Barbara contacted the office to let them know she wasn't returning, a condition Mark assumed would solidify his role in the office. But now there's a big conflict as both Melissa and Jake can barely stand to work together."

In this story, the mediator is hearing the final stages, but the "and ever since" part is yet to be decided. Can you see the steps, and how leaving any of them out or mixing them up might have made for a more confusing story?

Consider the box office hit *Avatar*, and how it follows the story spine:
Once upon a time there was a paraplegic Marine called Jake Sully with a traumatic past, who was just getting by in life. Every day he mourned the tragic death of his brilliant and talented brother.

But one day, he gets the opportunity to join a mission to distant moon Pandora. Because of that, he is promised surgery that will allow him to walk again in exchange for gathering info on the species that lives on the planet, the Na'Vi.

Because of that, he spends more time with them, eventually developing a real love for their world as well as for the beautiful Neytiri. Because of that love, he is unable to take part in the (soon-to-be-discovered) exploitative nature of the expedition, until finally, a full-blown war breaks out between humans and the Na'Vi. Finally, the battle is won, and Pandora is saved. And ever since then, Jake has lived in peace on Pandora.

Naturally, there are many details and elements missing here, but the spine is intact and is partly responsible for a story that is engaging and plays out in a way the audience expects. The story spine applies to any kind of story or narrative, written, spoken or cinematic, big or small. The fundamentals, once in place, can be reworked in literally endless ways.

Inside Stories

In any conversation, there is a high point. There might be multiple memorable points, but by definition, one part is the best and highest.

This can take many different forms. You can

share a big laugh. You can both get emotional and cry. You share a strong perspective on an issue that no one else does. You witness something either horrifying or hilarious together. You both struggle not to laugh when you observe something. You finish each other's sentences. Most of the time, if you do it correctly, your stories become high points because of the emotional impact and pure intrigue you can use them to create. This makes it easy because you are planting the seed of connection for you to harvest later.

Coincidentally, calling back to this high point later is what a deconstructed *inside joke* looks like. Therefore, to easily create an inside joke, all you have to do is refer to the high point later in the conversation. Take note of it and put it in your pocket for use in the near future. It's solid gold!

Don't let it go sour like month-old milk that you're afraid to throw away because of the smell. Assuming that you told a good story or elicited a good story earlier in the conversation, all you need to do is refer to it in the context of your current topic. Do you remember the previous chapter about creating commonalities? Well, using "call backs" to your own conversation is a perfect way to do this.

For example, you told a story about your favorite kind of dog earlier in the conversation. There was a high point about comparing yourself to a wiener dog because your shape makes it unavoidable.

Now your current topic of conversation is fashion, personal style and different types of jackets. How do you call back to the wiener dog high point by referring to it in the context of jackets? *"Yeah, unfortunately, I can't wear that type of jacket because I'm mostly similar to the wiener dog, remember?"*

Bring up the first topic, hopefully the topic of your story, and then use it in the current subject. You are repeating the old topic in a new context, and this tends to be better received, even if it wasn't funny the first time. And the best part is that you can keep doing this with the same thing to create an even stronger unique bond (inside joke!).

Listen for something funny or notable that you would classify as a conversational high point. Keep it in your pocket. Wait like a cheetah in the tall grass of the savannah to see a different context or topic you can repeat it in. And then unleash it.

Here's another example.

Prior conversational high point: a story about hating parking lots.

Current topic of conversation: the weather.

Callback: *Yeah, the rain will definitely be welcome when we can't find parking spots within ten blocks of our apartment.*

And here's one more:

Prior conversational high point: a story about loving donuts.

Current topic of conversation: hating work.

Callback: Well what if your office provided free donuts? How many would you need to change your opinion of work?

In the same way an orchestra conductor can hit the same high musical motif through different arrangements and songs, you can keep referring to this conversation high point. Voila, you've just created an inside joke from thin air. And in doing so, you've not only cemented a feeling of connection, but you've demonstrated loud and clear to your conversation partner that you're actually paying attention—I don't need to tell you how many brownie points this wins in real life.

Ask for Stories

Most of the focus with stories is usually on *telling* them—but what about soliciting them from others and allowing them to feel as good as you do when a story lands well? What about stepping aside and giving other people the spotlight (an underrated skill in conversation and life in general)?

If you are coming at a conversation from an egotistical place, you might see it as a way to dominate attention, make others like or admire you, or simply direct the topic in ways that work for you. But if you see conversation as something that's mutually enjoyable for everyone involved, then you suddenly don't care as much about *who's* talking, and what they're saying, but rather that the conversation itself is positive and flowing.

When we think about being good conversationalists, we almost always imagine the things we say, and how we say them. But it's just as important to *share* attention and focus, so it flows back and forth. How do you graciously invite others to take the limelight?

Well, it's just a matter of how you ask for other's stories. There are ways to make people gab for hours, and approaches where people will feel compelled to give a terse one-word answer.

For instance, when you watch sports, one of the most illogical parts is the post-game or post-match interview. These athletes are still caught in the throes of adrenaline, out of breath, and occasionally drip sweat onto the reporters. It's not a situation conducive to good stories, or even answers.

Yet when you are watching a broadcaster interview an athlete, does anything odd strike you about the questions they ask? The interviewers are put into an impossible situation and usually walk away with decent soundbites—at the very least, not audio disasters. Their duty is to elicit a coherent answer from someone who is mentally incoherent at the moment. How do they do that?

They'll ask questions like "So tell me about that moment in the second quarter. What did you feel about it and how did the coach turn it around then?" as opposed to "How'd you guys win?" or "How did you turn this match around, come back, and pull out all the stops to grab the victory at the very end?" as opposed to "How was the comeback?"

The key? They ask for a story rather than an answer. They phrase their inquiry in a way that can *only* be answered with a story, in fact.

Reporters provide the athletes with detail, context, and boundaries to set them up to talk as much as possible instead of providing a breathless one-word answer. It's almost as if they provide the athletes with an outline of what they want to hear and how they can proceed. They make it easy for them to tell a story and simply engage. It's like if someone asks you a question but, in the question, tells you exactly what they want to hear as hints.

Sometimes we think we are doing the heavy lifting in a conversation and the other party isn't giving us much to work with. But that's an excuse that obscures the fact we aren't making it easy for them, either. They might not be giving you much, but you also might be asking them the wrong questions, which is leading them to provide terrible responses. In fact, if you think you are shouldering the burden, you are definitely asking the wrong questions.

The truth about being a good conversationalist is that it's more like partner dancing than solo dancing—you need to work *with* your partner, prop them up, give them cues, and help things flow not just on your side, but on theirs too. Conversation can be much more pleasant for everyone involved if you provide fertile ground for people to work in. Don't set the other person up to fail and be a poor conversationalist; that will only make you invest and care less and cause the conversation to die out.

When people ask me low-effort, vague questions, I know they probably aren't interested in the answer. They're just filling the time and silence. To create win-win conversations and better circumstances for all, ask for stories the way the sports broadcasters do. Be considerate of how they are experiencing the conversation. Ask questions in a way that makes people want to share.

Stories are personal, emotional, and compelling. There is a thought process and narrative that necessarily exists. They are what show your personality and are how you can learn about someone. They reveal people's emotions and how they think. Last but not least, they show what you care about.

Compare this with simply asking for closed-ended answers. These answers are often too boring and routine for people to care. They will still respond to your questions but in a very literal way, and the level of engagement won't be there. Peppering people with shallow questions puts them in a position to fail conversationally.

It's the difference between asking "What was the best part of your day so far? Tell me how you got that parking space so close!" instead of just "How are you?"

When you ask somebody the second question, you're looking for a quick, uninvolved answer. You're being lazy and either don't care about their answer or want them to carry the conversational burden. When you ask somebody one of the first two questions, you're inviting them to tell a specific story about their day. You are encouraging them to narrate the series of events that made their day great or not. You are telling them that you're interested beyond the superficial. And your query can't really be covered with a one-word answer.

Another example is "What is the most exciting part of your job? How does it feel to make a difference like that?" instead of simply asking them the generic "What do you do?" When you only ask somebody what they do for a living, you know exactly how the rest of the conversation will go: "Oh, I do X. What about you?"

A final example is "How did you feel about your weekend? What was the best part? It was so nice outside," instead of just "How was your weekend?"

It might sometimes feel like asking a relatively closed question is more limiting than a broad, general one, and that you might be leading people toward a set outcome. It's a paradox, though: when you lead with a few set parameters and cues, you are actually helping the other person out. It's almost always easier to answer a more detailed, narrow question than it is to think of something to say to, "So, how are things?"

Prompting others for stories instead of simple answers gives them a chance to speak in such a way that they feel emotionally invested. This increases the sense of meaning they derive from the conversation. It also makes them feel you are genuinely interested in hearing their answer because your question doesn't sound generic.

Consider the following guidelines when asking a question:

1. Ask for a story
2. Be broad but with specific directions or prompts
3. Ask about feelings and emotions
4. Give the other person a direction to expand their answer into, and give them multiple prompts, hints, and possibilities
5. If all else fails, directly ask "Tell me the story about..."

Imagine that you want the other person to inform your curiosity. Other examples include the following:

1. "Tell me about the time you..." versus "How was that?"
2. "Did you like that..." versus "How was it?"
3. "You look focused. What happened in your morning..." versus "How are you?"

Let's think about what happens when you elicit (and provide) personal stories instead of the old, tired automatic replies.

You say hello to your coworker on Monday morning and you ask how his weekend was. At this point, you have cataloged what you will say in case he asks you the same. Remember, the person probably doesn't care about the actual answer ("good" or "okay"), but they *would* like to hear something interesting. But you never get the chance, because you ask him "How was your weekend? Tell me about the most interesting part—I know you didn't just watch a movie at home!"

He opens up and begins to tell you about his Saturday night when he separately and involuntarily visited a strip joint, a funeral, and a child's birthday party. That's a conversation that can take off and get interesting, and you've successfully bypassed the unnecessary and boring small talk that plagues so many of us.

Most people love talking about themselves. Use this fact to your advantage. Once someone takes your cue and starts sharing a story, make sure you are aware of how you're responding to that person through your facial expressions, gestures, body language, and other nonverbal signals. Listen for little details you can call back to later. Since there is always at least one exciting thing in any story, focus on that high point and don't be afraid to show that you're engaged.

One quick tip to show that you're involved and even willing to add to the conversation is something I call *pinning the tail on the donkey*. There is probably a better name for it, but it will suffice for the time being. The donkey is the story from someone else, while the tail is your addition to it. It allows you to feel like you're contributing, it makes other people know you're listening, and it turns into something you've created together. In essence, you are taking the impact that someone wants to convey, and you are amplifying it. You are assisting them in their own storytelling—they want to extract a specific reaction from you, and you are going above and beyond with the *tail*.

People will actually love you for it because, when you do this, your mindset becomes focused on assisting people's stories and letting them have the floor. Here's an example:

Bob's story: "I went to the bank and tripped and spilled all my cash, making it rain inadvertently."

Tail: "Did you think you were Scrooge McDuck for a second?"

When you make a tail, try to hone in on the

primary emotion the story was conveying, then add a comment that amplifies it. The story was about how Bob felt rich, and Scrooge McDuck is a duck who swims in pools of gold doubloons, so it adds to the story and doesn't steal Bob's thunder.

Sabrina's story: "After I ate lunch, I ran into the president of my company and he said he remembered me because of the great ideas I had at the last meeting!"

Tail: "Just like you were winning a beauty pageant!"

This story was about how Sabrina felt flattered and hopeful, and so the concept of a beauty pageant amplifies these emotions. Get into the habit of assisting other people's stories. It's easy, witty, and extremely appealing because you are helping them out.

Takeaways:

- Captivating people usually refers to telling a story that leaves them listening like children (in a good way). Storytelling is a big topic that is often made overly complex, but there are many ways of creating this feeling in small, everyday ways. To captivate others is no easy feat, but the material and ability lies within all of us. We just have to know where it is and how to access it.

- An easy way to imagine everyday storytelling is that your life is a series of stories—mini-stories, to be exact. Instead of giving one-word answers, get into the habit of framing your answers as a story with a point. It creates more engagement, lets you show your personality, and allows for smoother conversation. The bonus here is that you can prepare these before a conversation.

- The 1:1:1 method of storytelling is to simplify it as much as possible. The impact of a story won't necessarily be stronger if it is ten sentences versus two sentences. Therefore, the 1:1:1: method focuses on the discussion and reaction that occurs after a story. A story can be composed solely of (1) one action, (2) one emotion to be evoked, and (3) a one-sentence summary. Don't get lost rambling, and also make sure your listener feels that they are fully participating in the conversation.

- The story spine is more or less the formula for every movie that exists. It's a simple framework that you can use in your everyday stories and conversations, because it teaches you what emotional beats exist in a story. There is the status quo, the event that kicks things off, the set of consequences for changing the status quo, the climax or resolution, and then what happens after the fact.

- Stories can also be the basis for an inside joke. When you think about it, an inside joke is something that comes up multiple times with the same person and evokes a positive emotion. It's the same topic brought up in a different context. Thus, you just need to call back to a story through a conversation and there's a good chance it will stick as a "Remember when we talked about..." moment. The more you use it, the more a unique bond is created between only the two of you.

- Improving your storytelling ability is important, but what about eliciting stories from others? You can phrase your questions carefully to ask for stories rather than answers from people, which is a simple way to make conversation easier and more enjoyable for everyone involved. There are ways to make people open up to you and want to keep gabbing. Remember the lesson we learned with the 1:1:1 method in pinpointing the emotions that people are trying to evoke. To amplify this, you can *pin the tail on the donkey* and strategically add on to people's stories.

Chapter 4. Keep It Flowing and Smooth

Yes, small talk and all of its incarnations are quite dreadful as a whole. Yes, it can be awkward to get going sometimes, and few people really enjoy a conversation with a stranger that has to start "cold." But that doesn't change the fact that we are at least partially responsible for the outcomes we've gotten so far.

The reason most people hate small talk is not that they dislike conversation, or people, or conversation with people. Rather, they dislike the possibility of landing in one of those uncomfortable, boring chats with others that leave you feeling like you want the ground to open up and swallow you. The problem is when small talk *stays* small.

In a way, the best small talk in the world is always just an opening act for better things. If you're really good at small talk, then the joke is that you seldom have to do it that much, because when you do it right, it usually carries you away to deeper and more interesting conversation. On the other hand, if you hate small talk and avoid it, you become less skilled at it, and you set up a vicious cycle where you never learn to work small talk to your advantage.

What can we do to keep small talk from going stale and heading to a place where none of the people involved want to go? Sometimes it's like watching a slow descent into a black hole—you know where you're going, and it seems like there is nothing you can do about it other than ride it out.

So here are a few more ways to keep small talk anything but small.

Create Motion

You might not think about it this way, but conversations and interactions must always be moving somewhere; there must always be a sense of motion. It's about flow. When someone says, "Oh, we can talk on the phone for hours without even noticing it." they are saying that the conversation flows so well that the passage of time is irrelevant—the opposite of those excruciating awkward conversations where thirty seconds feels like a lifetime! When things flow and move at a good pace, we experience them as pleasurable and interesting.

When you have motion in a conversation, it's not that you are necessarily injecting it with energy and high spirits. It's that you can't stay on the same topic forever, and the conversation needs to evolve in one way or another, or else interest will be lost. It can go deeper, wider, broader, more specific, or onto another topic altogether. But if you stay stagnant and without motion, then... well... what are you doing?

That sounds something like the following: *"So yeah, you drove an hour to get here? That's crazy... Traffic is crazy. But everyone has commutes these days. What kind of traffic was there today?"*

That's an interaction with zero motion, and you can sense it. Let's look at this in a theatrical context. Let's suppose that the starting topic for a scene is a visit at the dentist, and it begins in the lobby. Does the scene stay in the lobby? Absolutely not. It moves in at least one of a few ways.

The scene might move locations into the

office of the dentist itself.

The scene might introduce multiple different characters.

The scene might change its focus and move away from the dentist altogether.

The scene might change the initial purpose, and the patient is visiting the dentist because he is an assassin, rather than to get his teeth cleaned. And so on. But the lobby is only a part of the story, and motion dictates that it be only temporary.

Contrast any of those situations to a scene that stays exactly in the same lobby, with the same characters, talking about the same thing. It may not be the worst scene, but it would have to be written *pretty damn well* to be interesting. And we know that's never the case with small talk.

We've already seen why stories are so compelling—and this is no different. For us to care about a conversation, it has to be alive and kicking. It has to feel like it has purpose and direction. This is why, strangely, it can be more satisfying to talk to someone who disagrees with you rather than one who shares the exact same opinion. When two people have precisely the same point of view, their conversation might not feel as dynamic as one where people are arguing or debating a little.

To boil this section down to one main sentiment, small talk and conversation in general goes much better if you intentionally create motion and seek to end up in a different place from where you started. For example, you can't talk about the weather forever. You need to create motion away from it, or into it from a different angle. You can plan for your conversations to resemble stories and movies, and learn about specific types of motion you can introduce on the fly.

When you go to a movie, you're not looking for something that fits your daily life. You're looking for a story about something significant, or unusual or extraordinary, a deviation from your everyday experience. If you're going to watch a biographical movie, you wouldn't want to watch the mundane parts of the characters' lives where they use the bathroom and brush their teeth.

Instead, you want to see the unique, interesting, and exaggerated moments. You want to see conflict, problem solving, then resolution. These are all accomplished by creating motion in normal conversation topics, and not just staying in one place.

A conversation that stays in one place will eventually become boring filler, since topics can easily be exhausted without motion. You might get the overwhelming feeling of covering the same ground, or have a nagging sense of "so what?" as you or the other person speaks. As I mentioned before, there are only so many comments or questions you can make about the weather. So, how do you create motion in a topic such as the weather?

Types of motion:

- Shift to a topic related to the weather.
- Go deeper into the topic of weather, beyond shallow and surface level comments.
- Share a personal experience with weather.
- Ask what their favorite types of weather are.
- Talk about the emotions the weather invokes in you.
- Discuss your nuanced opinion on the weather.
- Ask outlandish hypothetical questions about the weather.
- Reference third parties (papers, articles, statements from friends) regarding the

weather.

Note that these are similar ways of creating motion as the methods of manipulating the scene at the dentist's lobby from earlier. They force the interaction to go somewhere, and don't allow it to remain on comments about the weather, or to stay in the dentist's lobby.

Stagnation is one of the sneakier causes of poor interactions because it's something we all default to eventually. It's the lazy person's way of conversing—relying on the other person to shoulder the burden of topics and details. On the other hand, you might fall into a stagnant conversation because you're anxious and not fully present. While you should be paying attention to not letting the conversation die, your thoughts might be somewhere else entirely.

The rule of creating motion battles stagnation as it forces you to move away from lazy routines. Before one topic is completely bled dry, you can jump to other ones to keep engagement high and prevent dead ends and boredom. Think of yourself as a little bird jumping from one lily pad to the next, before your current one sinks under the water. You don't want to be in the position of trying to find the next lily pad after you've already started sinking!

Joseph Campbell was an Ivy League academic who studied the major myths of all the world's major spiritual traditions, and according to Campbell, the great myths and stories share certain elements in common. Regardless of whom the stories are told to, they are always effective because they hit on certain classic themes that are contained in the Hero Cycle.

No story contains a hero who is just a hero at the start and that's that. A hero's story is one that *moves* through initiation, challenge, success, and so on. The hero of the story starts at point A, and a situation arises that compels the hero to travel to point B. On the way back from point B to point A, certain conflicts and resolutions occur, and the hero is forever transformed and enlightened.

According to Campbell, people respond to the Hero Cycle because we can relate to the stages. We have all struggled, conquered, and grown through fear, adversity, and obstacles. It's what gives stories—and our lives—a sense of meaning and direction. The Hero Cycle goes a long way in explaining how people from all over the world, from all sorts of cultures, class levels and educational backgrounds, deal with the same phenomena in much the same way. It also explains why we're all intrigued by the same sorts of stories.

Great conversations are journeys. They never remain in the same place. There is a sense of direction, there is a sense of conflict that needs resolution, and there is a sense of tension that needs to be unwound. You don't end up in one preset place, but you do achieve closure. There's a payoff, and that's what creating motion does. Can you imagine how pointless and boring it would be to watch a movie where the main character just sort of... has a nice time? No stakes, no action, no threat or conflict, no change, no lesson, no reward, no mystery, no triumph, nothing. What would be the point of watching such a movie, right?

Let's take another example where the topic is suddenly steak.

Types of motion:

- What made you bring up steak and why it was on your mind?
- What memories you have with steak.
- How your view of steak has changed over the years.

- A random fact or piece of trivia you know about steak.
- Your emotions regarding steak.
- Ask for their emotions regarding steak.

We can dig deeper into the topic of steak, see it from another perspective entirely, examine some neighboring ideas, or take a leap and talk about the opposite of steak (that's an interesting question, what *is* the opposite of steak anyway?). The idea is that steak as a topic can only sustain conversation for so long. Eventually, you need to move and find more fuel.

It seems obvious that an interaction infused with motion must be heading somewhere, but many people will fall prey to one major trap. In the quest for motion, there is the danger of planning ahead with fixed ideas and destinations in mind.

This is dangerous for a few reasons.

First, imagine the concept of a performance with three participants, and all three already have fixed ideas of where they want the scene to go. In essence, they will be influencing each other and trying to herd the other two into the directions they want. It won't be pretty unless you like hearing three monologues simultaneously.

Second, you run the risk of spectacular failure when you are derailed from the path of your fixed destination. This is because you are so fixated on where you want to go that you haven't kept an open mind to other subjects or topics, and won't be able to adapt very well.

If you've been thinking the whole time about how to turn the conversation or performance to the subject of cars, you will probably come up tongue-tied when the subject instead turns to different types of hats. If you are open to the destination, you can roll with the punches, so to speak, because your mental bandwidth isn't otherwise consumed.

Have you ever been in a group conversation where someone suddenly and quite randomly interjects with a story that would have been relevant ten minutes ago, before the whole conversation moved on? They were so dead set on getting their piece said that they spoke whether it fit the flow or not. The conversation might splutter and stall as people realize that the person wasn't paying attention at all, but merely waiting for a gap so they could launch into their story. Not good!

Third, having a fixed destination in mind for your conversation makes you too goal-oriented, and by definition this means you are willfully ignoring everything else that happens in front of you. You might even be dismissing your conversation partner and their opinions because they aren't providing what you are looking for.

Suppose that you want to arrive at the same topic of cars, and other subjects keep getting in the way. Being overly goal-oriented would lead you to continually bring up cars, even though it would be a completely random shift in topic, and unwelcome since it was steered away from multiple times. It makes you appear tone deaf, and people will begin to wonder if you've even heard them speak. This tendency also generally makes you a fairly un-engaging conversationalist.

Instead, simply understand when you are being stagnant and lingering on the same topic and the same angle for too long. Remember, it's not about *you*, really, but about the conversation itself. Is it a strong, healthy, happy conversation that can flow easily?

Think on Your Feet

Now we know we need to create motion, and yet still, there are times when we are just stuck. Our minds go blank. It's not that we forget to change things up, just that we *can't*. When we try to think of different things to talk about, our dilemma becomes even worse, like trying to climb out of quicksand. The struggle just makes it tougher. We might become painfully aware of ourselves floundering, and that in itself is awkward. Before you know it, anxiety and pressure start to build, and you're beginning to sweat on your upper lip.

So let's simplify conversation.

Conversation is a series of statements, stories, and questions. After one person contributes one of those elements, the other person responds in kind, either on the same exact topic, or a topic that is in some way related to the original one. That's really it. Sometimes we'll have trouble thinking of what to say on the same topic, or finding a connection to another subject.

That's where free association comes in. *Isn't conversation just a series of free-association exercises?*

For instance, if someone started talking about motorcycles and you had no experience or impression of motorcycles, then what is your response going to be? You might not have anything to say about motorcycles, but what if you took away the statement and context and focused on the word and concept of motorcycles?

With simple free association, you can find a way to quickly and efficiently breathe new life into the conversation, regardless of how deeply stuck it may feel.

Just free associate five things about motorcycles. In other words, blurt out five things (nouns, locations, concepts, statements, feelings, words) that flashed into your brain when you heard the word "motorcycles." Allow your mind to go blank and zero in on the word "motorcycles." Stop thinking of the word as a trigger to past experiences and memory. Instead, start looking at it as a fresh concept unconnected to what you've experienced before.

Play a word association game with yourself. What does "motorcycles" make you think of? We're just talking about purely intellectual connections.

It doesn't matter what you feel, what your emotions are. It doesn't matter what your experiences were, whether you were traumatized or not. It has nothing to do with that. This is just a purely intellectual challenge to try to rapidly fill out a list of what "motorcycles" as a concept can connect to.

Let's switch words. For most people, when the word "cats" is mentioned, they think of kittens, cuddles, sand boxes, cheetahs, lions, fish, sushi, fur, dogs, allergies, the musical, etc. Keep in mind that there is no right or wrong answer here. It's all free association. What's important is that you're rapidly filling out that list of things that you can intellectually connect with the word "cats."

You'll notice that doing this is much easier than coming up with a responsive statement or question to the declaration, "I love cats." Yet, your task and challenge is exactly the same—where do you go with what the other person said? With that framework and perspective, it's much easier to disassociate from the actual statement and free associate with the subject matter.

Doing this will train your brain to think

outside the box, approach conversation in a non-linear way, and see the many possible directions one simple concept or word can take you. The trick is that free association works best when you're relaxed. If you're anxiously telling yourself "quick, think of something original, or else," you're likely working against yourself!

Now suppose that someone proclaimed their love for car racing, and suppose that you know nothing about that either. What are the top five or six free associations that come to mind for car racing?

For me, it's a mixture of (1) NASCAR, (2) gas, (3) tires, (4) *The Fast and the Furious* movies, (5) Japan (don't ask me), (6) Mustangs. Here's the magic part: each of these six associations are perfectly normal topics to switch to while remaining in the flow of the conversation.

"I love watching car racing! It's so fun!"

"You mean like NASCAR, or illegal street racing?"

"I always wondered what kind of gas mileage those cars get."

"Do those cars have specialized tires? I don't

think my car's tires could take that!"

"So are *The Fast and the Furious* movies your favorites?"

"I heard they do some kind of drift racing in Japan—do you mean like that?"

"I always imagine car racing happens with huge, powerful Mustangs. Is that the kind of car races you watch?

Here you can see something interesting: you don't need to know anything at all about the topic to free associate about it. You don't have to be an expert. If you were chatting to a biology PhD who casually mentioned "psychobiotics," you might smile and say, "Oh gosh, what is *that*? Sounds to me like some kind of hallucinogenic yogurt!"

Here, the fact that you are ignorant about the topic means nothing—you can still engage in a lively and personable way in the conversation (and invite the other person to speak more about what they know).

If you have some weird or nonsensical associations, all the better. There's a chance for a little humor, creativity, and an opportunity to bring some of your own emotion and personality into the mix. You might not feel like a naturally witty or humorous person, but practice free association often enough and you might surprise yourself with what you come up with!

Try free association with the words "coffee" and "trains" and think about how much easier it is to construct questions and generally converse about something once you can form a mental map of the topic and its related topics.

You just feel *unstuck*.

Of course, the best way to do this is not to try it for the first time when you're in an actual conversation. Practice free association consciously several times throughout the course of a week. The more you do it, the better you get at it.

Here's how to practice: on a piece of paper, write five random words. They can be anything—a noun, verb, memory, or even an emotion or feeling. Suppose the first word you write is "napkin." As quickly as possible, write three associations for that word. Take the last word you came up with, and then as quickly as possible, write three associations for that new word. Repeat three times, and then move to the next set of words.

Napkin   -> table, spoon, fine dining.
Fine dining -> France, Michelin Star, butler.
Butler   -> Jeeves, white gloves, Michael Jackson.
And so on.

Or pick a word at random from a dictionary, and list out fifteen words in a free-association word chain as quickly as possible. Then, do it again and again—verbally, because that will require the quickest thinking.

After you grow more comfortable with random free association with words, you can take the next step and choose two random words from a dictionary and pretend they are the name of a company. Then, create a short story about what that company does, as quickly as possible.

For example, the two random words you pick are: bottle, Africa. The short story I would construct about a company named "Africa Bottle" is that they import African homemade liquors.

The final step of this set of free-association exercises is to choose five random words from the dictionary and make up a story that involves all of the words, as quickly as possible.

Again, these exercises are intended to train you to think quickly and be creative, so it's imperative that you do these exercises at "full speed." They'll be tough, and at first, your responses might seem terrible. But, imagine how big the difference will be between your first day and your tenth day, for example. That's the power of free association, and practice.

If you also care to analyze the similarities between free association and conversation, you might find that they are virtually the same. In conversation, you'll reply to someone on a topic, a slightly related topic, or a new topic. That's exactly the type of thought process that free association takes. In a sense, free association trains you to come up with conversation topics quickly.

Practicing free association is an excellent foundation for good conversation because conversation is about relating unrelated things, making connections, and going with the flow of topics. Next time you're struggling for something to say, take a step back and tap into your previously practiced free-association skills.

Just as with every other aspect of conversation skills, you can only master it if you try it enough times. The best part of all this is that you can do it instantly. You get caught in a stream of consciousness flow. Always remember there is no right or wrong answer. If you believe there is, you'll be putting unnecessary pressure on yourself. Remove that pressure, and you open up a whole world of fresh possibilities.

Helpful Acronyms

HPM, SBR, and EDR. What are these strange acronyms?

Put simply, they are nine distinct types of responses you can use for practically any topic that arises in a conversation. They are all quite helpful because if you are stumped or you can see an awkward silence creeping around the corner, you can essentially use them as ice-breaking cue cards to find topics to talk about, and ways to respond to people.

It also makes sense to refer to them as a "plug and playable" because all you need to do is plug in one of these responses and bingo—it just works.

The right responses can go a long way to jump-start and add new life to your conversations. It doesn't matter how good a conversationalist you are because awkward silences are always lurking around the corner. Using these acronyms, you can always find a way to work around these impending conversation killers.

HPM

HPM stands for History, Philosophy, and Metaphor.

This means in response to a question or statement directed at you, you reply with your own statement that evokes history, philosophy, or a metaphor.

HPM tends to draw on your memories, experiences, and opinions, which is a bit different from the other acronyms you'll be learning about in this chapter. It's more internal and personal, while others are more external and in the moment.

History means you reply with your personal experience regarding a topic (no, don't trawl your memory for an exciting anecdote about life in medieval times). For example, if someone tells you a story about skiing, this is a prompt for you to reply with:

- That reminds me of the last time I skied...
- That's just like the first time I skied as a child...
- What a coincidence, my mother's friend went skiing last week and had a blast...

Philosophy, on the other hand, involves your personal stance, take, or opinion on a specific topic (again, this is not to say you need to share your knowledge about Spinoza's *Ethics*!). This is where you share personal or emotional material. For example, if someone tells you that same rousing story about skiing, you can reply with:

- I've always loved skiing because...
- I've hated skiing ever since...
- Skiing is so fun! My favorite hobby.
- I don't know how I feel about skiing. On one hand...

Metaphor, on the other hand, involves what the conversation topic reminds you of. If you're hearing the same story about skiing for the third time in the same day, you might not want to talk about it again. Thus, this is a prompt for you to subtly change the topic to something that's related or ... not so related.

If you've been practicing your free association, this kind of thing will come as second nature. It works as long as you can preface it with some sort of transition.

- That reminds me of …
- That's just the opposite of snowboarding, isn't it?
- That makes me think of…
- Isn't that similar to…

Keep in mind that HPM is more focused on you, what you think, and what your experiences are. It really has nothing to do with the other person, but with what the topic at hand evokes from you—a memory, an opinion or feeling, or a jumping-off point from which to change the subject.

Seems pretty easy and intuitive, right? The point is that everyone has these things—everyone has personal stories and experiences, everyone has opinions and stances on subjects, and everyone can envision how one topic is related to or reminiscent of another. It's just that we are lazy conversationalists who don't realize the broad scope of what's available for us to talk about.

SBR, on the other hand, is similar but

probably easier to use quickly on your feet than HPM. It's external, which means everything that you need to continue any conversational topic is right there in front of you.

SBR

SBR stands for Specific, Broad, and Related. To any statement or question directed to you, you can reply with one of these types of statements.

Specific involves asking targeted questions regarding the topic you're talking about. This kind of response allows you to drag the conversation forward or take it deeper by pulling out fine details. Suppose you want to get into the nitty-gritty of what's being discussed. Let's take the skiing story example we used earlier:

- What kind of slopes did you go down?
- How was the snow?
- How many times have you skied recently?

Broad means you ask broad questions about the topic. These create context and are great springboards to sub-topics. This enables the conversation to proceed smoothly from the main topic to a sub-topic and all the way to a completely new topic. Get the background and the general lay of the land here.

- Where was this?
- Who did you go with?
- When was this?
- How did you drive there?

Finally, related refers to asking about something that is either directly or broadly related to the subject of your conversation. The great thing about "related" is that it allows you to explore issues tangential to the overall topic.

- I love when it's snowing outside.
- I love taking weekend trips.
- Isn't it great, getting physically active as much as possible?

The unifying characteristic of the SBR conversation strategy is that it focuses primarily on the topics you're talking about. That is, you're taking the exact topic that's in front of you, digging deeper into it, and essentially letting the other person guide you through questions.

So that was a fairly direct and straightforward set of rules, right? Now you have six responses you can pop into just about any situation, almost as if you're reading off of cue cards and can just say "Oh, hmm... philosophy... well, the way I feel about that is...."

Onto the last: EDR. With these final three of the nine frameworks, you've added a whole lot of engagement, personalization, depth, and intrigue to a conversation that might otherwise have begun and ended at "Hey, how was your weekend?"

EDR

EDR is the last part of the nine frameworks that you can employ to answer just about anything. It straddles HPM and SBR—you can use what's in front of you, but it's even better if you draw internally and speak about your own thoughts and opinions.

EDR stands for Emotion, Detail, and Restatements.

E (emotion) means when you respond to a statement made in conversation, you state someone else's emotion or emotional state.

You mention what you believe your conversational partner's emotional response to be. For example, "It seems like you're really excited about that." If it's not 100 percent apparent and clear to you what the other person's emotional state is, you can make a statement summing up an assumption to see whether you're right or not. You don't have to be correct; the point is that whether you are or not, they will correct you and automatically explain their actual feelings.

"I went skiing last weekend!"

"You sound really excited about that."

If you were wrong... "Actually, I'm not. Here's why..."
If you were right... "Totally, it's very thrilling to be on the slopes."

Think of this like being a very open-minded counselor who just wants to talk about other people's feelings. When you state someone's emotions, you appear to be very in tune with them and engaged in their well-being.

What makes this approach particularly effective is that you talk about other people's emotions, not yours.

As we've established, people like to be the center of attention. The more attention you give them, the more they're likely to talk.

With E, you allow them to take the limelight and express their emotions. People appreciate this because most people like to feel they matter, and they aren't often given a chance to feel that way.

D (detail) means when you respond to a topic, you do so by asking for details and how they relate to the person with whom you're speaking. This is similar to the S in SBR.

You get the details and you also get an overview of how they impact the person you're speaking to. For example, the key journalistic "5 Ws" (who, what, where, when, and why) work perfectly here. The 5 Ws work so well because they allow you to tie in different details to the person with whom you're speaking. Think of yourself as a detective sifting through different clues to solve a mystery.

For example, "When did you start doing that?" "How did that make you feel?" and so on.

R (restatements) means restating or summarizing what the other person said and then throw it back at them.

This is very effective because it lets the

person you're speaking with know loud and clear that you're paying attention to them. You're paying so much attention that you can't get their words out of your mouth!

As I mentioned above, people like to feel they matter. What better way to show that appreciation than simply letting them know, in clear terms, that you were listening to what they had to say, and moreover, you want to make sure you understand what they've said.

When you restate what they say, you are essentially validating them twice. First, the simple act of summarizing what they said already validates them. It lets them know that you were listening to them. On top of that, you ask for their permission or confirmation to see if you've understood them correctly. This creates a tremendous sense of comfort and validation for the other person.

"I went skiing in the mountains last weekend."

"So you went skiing in the *mountains* last weekend?"

"So you went *skiing* in the mountains last weekend?"

"So you went skiing in the mountains *last weekend*?"

This prompts them to elaborate on their statement without your having to say much. All you did was say the exact same thing back to them, with a slight emphasis on a different word to indicate that you are curious and want clarification on an aspect of what they've said. Each of these three versions is a distinctly different assertion or question, but you are using their exact words.

Think of this like a psychologist prompting a patient for deeper and more personal discoveries and insights. By using EDR in addition to HPM and SBR, you now have nine ways to respond to people about anything.

Which of the nine feel easy and natural to you, and which feel difficult?

Pay careful attention, because as previously noted, some of these are more about your own thoughts and internal workings, and others are about the situation in front of you and the other person. So if you skew too much in one direction, it can mean you're either a conversational narcissist or someone who provides no value or substance.

Chain them together, and with these nine techniques you will pretty much never run out of things to talk about.

Takeaways:

- How can you keep conversation, small talk especially, flowing smoothly when you don't feel like you have anything to talk about? This is a challenge even with good friends sometimes. Most of the time, this feeling of stagnancy occurs because you are doing exactly that—stagnating—and nothing is being added or extracted from the interaction on either side. But there are several ways you can change that.
- First, create a sense of motion. Staying on the same topic, sentiment, or feeling for too long will create a feeling of boredom and even mild stress. *Why can't you escape it?* Indeed, if you watch a movie and it's just people talking the entire time, the movie better be *damn well written* to be interesting. To contrast, Joseph Campbell's hero's journey is a classic story that follow someone's quest, success, and subsequent transformation. Luckily, there are a multitude of ways to create motion in an interaction, but the most powerful part is simply realizing that things must

move in some way.

- Sometimes, despite knowing full well that we must create motion, we are unable to do it. Sometimes our minds go blank. The next couple of sections deal with this specifically—how can you think more quickly on your feet? This requires practice; no one who manages it consistently is truly born with such a quick wit. And so how do you practice it? With free association, by simply taking a word and naming a few words or concepts that it reminds you of. The important part is to train your brain's quick response reflex and break through any mental filters you might possess. You can also choose two words and relate them with a brief story, or flip to random words in the dictionary and use them to create a story.
- Finally, in case all else escapes your mind, there are three incredibly helpful acronyms that can assist you in never running out of things to say on the fly. These are: HPM, SBR, and EDR. HPM stands for History (your personal experience with the topic), Philosophy (your opinion on the topic), and Metaphor (what the topic makes you think of). SBR stands for Specific (more detail on the topic), Broad (broader context of topic), and Related (related topics). EDR stands

for Emotion (the emotions the topic evokes in the other person), Detail (more detail on the topic), and Restatements (restating the topic to prompt greater elaboration).

Chapter 5. Go Deeper, Be Better

Up to this point of the book, we've talked about initial impressions, storytelling, and how you should generally approach people to bypass small talk.

Let's focus a bit more now on how to really get to that next level of closeness with someone. It's not as hard as you might imagine, but it may require some tweaking of the way you currently interact with people. This is more or less a chapter on how to get into someone's good graces. We will first talk about compliments, a more obvious method, while the other sections cover imparting comfort, safety, and ease. Some of this might seem simple or obvious, but it's still not being put to good use by most of us!

The Oldest Trick in the Book

Certainly one of the easiest ways to get into someone's good graces is to compliment quickly and freely. This is ground zero for flattery and making people light up with a smile. If you think about it, you probably have positive thoughts about people running through your head all day, so there's no reason not to simply give voice to them. We just tend to fixate on sneer-worthy aspects more than we like.

Within the world of compliments, there are two levels I want to differentiate between. The first level is the low-hanging fruit—there are only so many times someone can hear that they have nice eyes and still be impacted by it. This level is what most people are stuck on. They are more likely to be simple observations rather than in-depth statements.

You'll know the difference between the two types of compliments by the impact they have on the person. Eyes are great—but it's something rather shallow to point out. There are only so many times you can hear that you have nice eyes and still care. How do you give compliments that are more thoughtful and less superficial?

The second level of compliment goes below the surface. For maximum impact, compliment people for two things (besides the obvious and superficial). Compliment people on (1) things they have control over and (2) things they have made a conscious choice about. There may be significant overlap between the two.

Why? Because these are the things that are most likely to make people feel proud and recognized. If you have beautiful eyes, well, that's lucky I guess, but it's not an achievement or something you had a say in. It's not something that tells you anything about your character, so it can feel hollow. This is why very attractive people can almost become immune to compliments about their appearance—they know how little they had to do to be attractive, so it doesn't feel like a real compliment to them at all.

For instance, no one has control over the color of their eyes; thus, it's not a very impactful compliment. However, someone may have made a very conscious choice to wear a specific hairstyle that takes an hour to get ready. If you compliment this, you are telling them you recognize and praise their effort. If you compliment their outfit, you are acknowledging their awesome taste. Other examples include specific habits, words and phrases people use, distinct fashion sense, unique thoughts, and so on.

Why are these aspects so much more personal and impactful to compliment? Because they reflect the person's thought processes and identity. These are choices people consciously make to represent themselves—their tastes and values. They don't do it for others, but they are hoping to be judged positively and lauded for their choices. The more outrageous something might be, the more valuable positive confirmation is. Therefore, when you compliment someone on their choices and thoughts, you validate them to the highest degree. You're telling them that you agree with them, it was all worth it, and they made the right choice!

You can see that complimenting a person on something they don't have control over, such as their eye color, doesn't amount to much other than "Hey, congratulations on winning the genetic lottery with your eyes!" Now, if this person was wearing colored contacts, it might be a better compliment because that's obviously a choice they made to alter their original eye color.

Compliment things your conversation partner has obviously put some thought into. This might include a bright shirt, a distinctive handbag, an unusual piece of art, or a vintage car. These things are out of the ordinary, uncommon, and reflect a deliberate deviation from the norm. You never know if someone's persona is ingrained in the fact that they choose to wear Hawaiian shirts. By complimenting someone on something they've clearly chosen with purpose, you acknowledge and validate the statement they have chosen to make about themselves.

Other things you can compliment people on that show individual choice are their manners, the way they phrase certain ideas, their opinions, their worldview, and their perspective.

It's worth mentioning that your compliment actually has to be sincere. If you are complimenting someone just for the sake of saying something nice, it's usually quite transparent, and will have a poor effect on the person. Nobody likes to feel that they're being manipulated in this way. Which would you rather have: someone expressing a legitimate appreciation for you, or someone who is behaving in ways to deliberately make you feel good?

This is a subtle point that's worth driving home. Women especially may have experienced compliments from men as merely transactional, or a gateway to unwanted and insincere attention. Similarly, women might give people compliments because they're trying to bolster their self-esteem, cheer them up or curry favor. It's not uncommon for someone to simply say, "Oh, I love your shirt!" when what they really mean is "Oh, I see you've made an effort wearing that really strange shirt today. I want to be polite so I'll mention it and say it looks great." Big difference!

Make your compliments sincere, appropriate and respectful. Above all else, compliments trigger one of the most fundamental weaknesses humans have: we are starved for attention. We like to be put in the spotlight and given the attention that we feel we deserve. People aren't really complimented that much on a daily basis—especially men.

We can easily see this because most people don't know how to take a true and genuine compliment without a bit of awkward fumbling. Make it a goal to see people fumble about the compliments you give them—that means it impacts them more because they simply don't get many, and it will have a greater effect on your relationship. You want people to experience your compliment as genuine, rather than brush it off as inconsequential.

If someone is always complimented on one thing, can you compliment them on something else, something that they may actually feel underappreciated for?
On a related matter, try to make it a habit to notice, point out, and celebrate people's idiosyncrasies. Everyone has their own sort of either mental, emotional, or physical traits that make them uniquely *them*, and these can take unlimited forms.

You might think that these idiosyncrasies are things that people want to hide and conceal from others. But here's the surprise: when you notice, point them out, and celebrate them, they'll love you for it. In the context of conversation, it's going to be things like their mannerisms, tics, gestures, body language, vocabulary, unique phrasing, or even how they cross their legs. There is a multitude of other possibilities. You just have to make sure that you frame it in a unique, positive, and fascinated light.

For instance, everyone has a different physical ritual they engage in, mostly subconsciously, when they speak to others. If it's not a physical ritual during conversation, everyone has different ways they perceive and go about their day. Some people will chew fifty times for each mouthful of food. Others will avoid touching doorknobs when opening doors. And some might avoid stepping on cracks in the sidewalk for fun.

Once you have observed the same idiosyncrasy at least a few times to make sure it's not because of a mosquito or some other environmental factor, draw attention to it! Not in a negative manner, but in an observant one.

- *Hey, that's an interesting way of tying your shoes...*
- *I see that you keep twisting the jars into patterns. Tell me about that.*
- *Do you favor your left arm? You crack it five times every time we walk inside.*
- *Did you read* Nineteen Eighty-Four *recently? You use the word "goodplus" a lot...*

Make sure that you don't have any judgmental tone in your voice or body language when you point out an idiosyncrasy.

You're not calling them out. It's not negative. You're just shining the spotlight on something that is personal to them that they thought people might not notice. But you did notice. The fact that you did will make them feel special because you've apparently paid so much attention to them. To continue with the above examples, what do you imagine the response will be? Very likely pleasant shock and a compulsion to open up and elaborate themselves to you.

Next, we turn to something that should be so foundational as to be taught in school from childhood, and yet...

Two Ears, One Mouth

Raise your hand if this has ever happened to you: you are speaking with someone, and immediately after you finished speaking, they ignored absolutely everything you said, didn't even acknowledge it, and continued on a completely unrelated thought or tangent? It's as if they didn't hear a word of what you said, and they probably didn't.

Can you imagine this happening during a theater performance?

Actor #1: "I want to go to the butcher shop

now, so let's go!"

Actor #2: "This table is fascinating. Do you think it was made in Germany?"

Actor #1: "Uh... so back to that butcher shop..."

Actor #1 would be left confused and scrambling. Unfortunately, if we're honest with ourselves, this type of interaction is common and happens often. For all of our good intentions, most people are terrible listeners, us included, and it impacts the quality of our relationships. People want to say what they want to say, and they are more interested in their own lives than anyone else's. To most, on an unconscious level, *sharing* is caring, not listening.

This is normal human nature, but that doesn't mean it's best for us. Good habits such as self-discipline, willpower, and focusing on others explicitly goes against our built-in instincts, so it can take some undoing. Conversation is a two-way street, and you have to give the other person space to speak in order to receive it for yourself.

In today's frankly fragmented and fractured society, people no longer enjoy the deep kind of social connections they had before. We might feel like we are never listened to, never heard, never understood. This makes us unconsciously hog attention when we do have a conversation, but it's a vicious cycle—the other person responds by trying to grab it back, and so, instead of a genuine sharing of connection, we end up using dialogue as a kind of tug-of-war.

Unfortunately, many people (hopefully not you) can see conversation as a dumping ground. This will happen in one of two ways.

People will either come in with a fixed agenda and set of talking points, or they will be so wrapped up in their own lives that they just want to share with you and not hear about yours. In either case, they open their mouths, unload information, and don't stop until they get tired of their own voices. You are there primarily to receive the pre-prepared speech, or nod in agreement as they offload.

How does this make the listener feel? People aren't dumb. People can detect when you are engaged and interested in what they have to say, i.e. when you just want to talk *at* them, not *with* them.

They will get the distinct feeling that the other person is just waiting for their turn to speak and is not interested in anything they have to say. It's like they know they are doing their best to try to listen to you, but they feel that their lives are so much more captivating that they can't resist going back to that topic.

The listeners are not getting much out of the exchange, and at some point, only listening to someone and having your prompts ignored is burdensome and flat-out annoying. In a theater performance, the two parties won't be working together, and the scene will be disjointed as one person will have to keep catering to the other person's whims.

While most people hate to be on the receiving end of this, we could probably spend our energy more wisely by learning ways not to do this to others. Silence is an effective communication tool. Use it more frequently than you think you should. If anyone you engage with answers your questions happily but doesn't pause to ask you how you're doing, then *they* need to shut up more. If that's you, *you're* the one who needs to shut up.

It can be difficult because sometimes we build up a lot of steam during conversations. We feel like we're on a roll with what we're talking about, and we could keep going for hours. Maybe they say something and you just know you have an amazing story to respond with, and all of a sudden all you can think of is finding a place to wedge that story in.

That's a selfish pursuit, and if someone wants to hog the spotlight for a while, you must absolutely surrender it and be willing to derail yourself and jump completely into someone else's ideas and topics.

Therefore, in conversation, one of the first keys is that you don't just wait for your turn to speak. To some, this sounds like "let people speak and don't interrupt them," but it goes deeper than that.

This actually means to empty your mind and stop composing your response or the next topic while someone is speaking. When you are listening, you aren't only waiting for your turn to speak and preparing for that. You are listening with a blank slate and *then* tailoring your response directly to what was just said, after they've said it. You aren't listening with an aim to respond. You are just listening, and then later, you are responding.

Wherever the other person wants to derail the conversation, you must be willing to go with them. That's great listening and a showing of respect.

If you are letting the other person speak simply because you feel like you shouldn't be talking for so long at one stretch, you are just waiting for your turn to speak. You aren't participating in the conversation; you are giving a monologue in the hopes that the other person contributes and listens to it. Or worse yet, the other person listens in a similar fashion to you and you are in a case of dueling monologues versus a dialogue.

Even more seriously, you are not respecting your conversation partner. Your behavior tells them you do not value them enough to listen while you are waiting for your turn to unload what you have to say. Much of this is subconscious, so it would be wrong to say that we are malicious in our daily conversations. We sometimes get too eager to talk about ourselves because our lives are most interesting to us, so why wouldn't they be to others?

We're like puppies discovering snow for the first time and are unable to contain our excitement.

We already had an example of poor listening earlier—that damned butcher shop.

However, it was egregious, and most examples of poor listening are subtler and you may not even realize they are a problem. They might merely be classified as "ineffective."

Ineffective listening:

Bob: I heard that butcher shop is pretty good.
Johnson: Oh, cool. Where is it?
Bob: About a ten-minute walk.
Johnson: Oh, I see. Did I tell you about my new niece?
Bob: No, you didn't. Congratulations.
Johnson: She's really cute. Here are some pictures.

The reason this is ineffective listening is because Johnson merely pays lip service to Bob's interests before being unable to contain himself from talking about his niece. He doesn't see Bob's thought to completion and cuts him off in the middle to shift to his own topic. This is the type of poor listening that we encounter more on a daily basis. It's subtle, but sometimes it's just as bad.

Here is that conversation but with better listening:

Bob: I heard that butcher shop is pretty good.

Johnson: Oh, cool. Where is it?

Bob: About a ten-minute walk.

Johnson: Oh, I see. Did you want to check it out?

Bob: I do. Do you want to come with me?

Johnson: Sure. Along the way, I can show you pictures of my new niece.

Both parties are able to wedge their thoughts in. Conversation that improves relationships and makes people feel positive about each other involves an interplay between silence and speaking, and both parties have an equal opportunity to take the spotlight.

Collaboration is the name of the game, and waiting for your turn to speak doesn't contribute to a shared goal—only yours.

Interrupting, of course, is also a no-no in the quest for better listening. Interrupting sends the message of "I know you were talking, but what I have to say is more interesting for both of us" or "What I'm saying is more important than what you say" or even, on a more unconscious level, "I am more important and worthy of speaking than you are." Again, it's not conscious, but that's what happens when we put our thoughts and agendas over those of other people.

You might not think it's a big deal, but if you keep interrupting, that is precisely the message you send. Your conversation partner doesn't know what's going on inside your head, so who can blame them for feeling alienated if your actions don't represent your intentions?

Here are a few quick guidelines for interruptions. First, don't interrupt others unless you agree with them so emphatically that you can finish their sentence with them. Second, if you do interrupt them for any reason, ask them immediately after you finish speaking what they were saying and bring it back to them. Acknowledge your error and quickly put the spotlight back onto them. Sometimes we can interrupt just because we were so excited by the story that we had to join in. Acknowledge this, though, and gracefully hand the conversation back, reiterating that you really want to hear what the other person was saying.

Third, try to abide by the two-second rule to police yourself. After someone finishes speaking, pause for a full two seconds while contemplating what they've said and externally demonstrate that you are analyzing their words. Then, and only then, may you reply. This will get you into the habit of thinking before speaking and addressing people first. Conversations will feel less rushed or pushy.

You can also get into the habit of using phrases that encourage others to keep speaking. It's not always enough to just shut up and nod your head. Staring blankly at someone will make people feel like they have to repeat themselves and that their message didn't get through. It has the same exact effect as not listening to them.

You have to demonstrate that you are mentally following every step of the conversation, even if you aren't. Use your facial expressions, eyebrows, gestures, and laughs to signal a reaction to each of their statements. Nod when they emphasize a point. Here are some encouraging phrases to show interest and investment:

- Uh-huh.
- I see.
- That's interesting.
- Tell me more.
- And then?
- What happened next?
- What about that?

If you look at conversations as simply an

exercise to be heard and shine a spotlight on your ego, you are doing a great disservice to everyone you engage with. Not everyone is as interested in your life as you are. Even if you think you are listening and shutting up sufficiently, there's a chance that you still cling to your train of thought subconsciously and are waiting for the opportunity to assert it.

To improve your conversations and connect better, you need to shut up more. As the old saying goes, you can't learn when you're speaking.

Though it may not seem that way at first, listening is actually one of the most self-interested things you can do, because you are the person who benefits and learns. You learn more about people, you sharpen your conversational skills, you endear yourself to others... and you let yourself off the hook of having to come up with interesting things to say all the time! It's a complete win-win situation.

To see the simple power of shutting up more, make your next conversation with a friend all about them. Try to find out about every minute detail of their day. This means you shutting up, listening to them, reacting accordingly, and asking questions that go deeper. Say as little as you can while reacting properly and moving the conversation along in whatever direction they want. Make it as unbalanced an exchange as possible.

Don't interrupt them, and try to coax as many stories from them as you can. Note how willing they are to speak about themselves in detail.

Is this easy or difficult for you? Did it feel unnatural to ask people deeply about their day and focus on them? If it did, then you just might need to practice shutting up more! Maybe, though, you realized that putting the focus on other people doesn't actually take away from any of the enjoyment of conversation—as a matter of fact, it may even enhance it.

By the way, much of what we've discussed regarding listening thus far is about how to resist your selfish tendencies to seize the spotlight and share to your heart's content. But if you have that tendency, so does the person across from you. Step aside and give *them* the chance to be selfish in an effort to better your communication.

Think about how you feel after you leave a

conversation where you don't share much. You probably feel neglected, suppressed, and like it was a negative experience because you weren't able to add your thoughts. Now imagine a scenario where you were given all the air space you could use and had a captive audience. You'd come away feeling good because you were able to articulate the subtleties of your thoughts. You know how good it feels to express and explain yourself, so don't rob others of that same experience.

Make people feel like you care and they matter. Giving people the spotlight is an entirely different thing from making sure people know they have the spotlight. Treat them as though they were the most interesting person in the room, and as if you are really grateful to learn more about them. Granted, a few people may take advantage of the opportunity to speak and proceed to chew your ear off. But more likely is that, in letting others speak, you deepen their positive feelings toward you and, eventually, they can relinquish the limelight again.

"You can make more friends in two months by becoming interested in other people than you can in two years by trying to get other people interested in you."—Dale Carnegie

Ask Better Questions

Finally, when it comes to going deeper, there's one certain way to do it: by wielding questions as shovels. A question is a powerful tool that brings together many of the concepts we've covered so far—a good question sets a great tone, finds common ground, captivates people, keeps things moving and shows others that you're paying attention.

Unfortunately, most questions we use just don't get anywhere. They're more of hammers and saws, which are not so well-suited for digging deeper. Some of them are made lazily, which prompts lazy answers in return. Others are plain confusing or meandering and without a clear purpose. Most of them aren't geared at looking beneath the surface and understanding people.

Good questions help both parties develop deeper communication. Well-constructed inquiries can prompt a respondent to find new ways to think about their situations, which strengthens trust and keeps communication fresh. Thankfully, asking good questions is a practice that's completely within your power.

Recall in the beginning of the book we discussed researcher Arthur Aron's 1997 study on personal questions fostering feelings of closeness. Although the questions were not offensively intrusive, they were more than just small talk ("Would you like to be famous and how?" "Do you have a secret hunch about how you will die?" "What is your most terrible memory?" "How do you feel about your relationship with your mother?").

Aron's findings were clear: going more deeply or intensely in our communications can create positive results far more swiftly than one might think. Coming up with effective questions isn't necessarily a reflexive act that we can do on the fly. To elicit more revealing answers that build depth and improve intimate relationships, here are six strategies that can be of great help in digging deep and learning about people.

These are most definitely not small-talk questions.

1. Ask open-ended questions. Questions that require only yes or no answers will usually produce nothing more than yes or no answers. If the question contains no prompt for the responder to elaborate, there's a very good chance they won't.

Open-ended questions, though, can spark discussions and bring up new, revelatory understandings that binary questions don't encourage. For example, instead of asking, "*Are you satisfied* with your relationship with your mother?" you could ask, "*Why is* your relationship with your mother the way it is? *How* did it get that way?"

These types of questions always seek to find reasons, stories, emotions, and patterns of thought. They are not asking for simple information in the form of facts. They are looking for the analysis and reaction before and after the fact.

2. Get behind assumptions. We all operate through our own personal experiences, knowledge, and assumptions—you know what you know. Good communication involves understanding *someone else's* beliefs. When they speak about issues that are unfamiliar to us, we ask them to explain what they mean, what they believe, or what assumptions they bring to the situation.

Well-worded questions can bridge that gap: "How did you come to that conclusion?" "What makes this particular situation different from normal?" "What gave you this idea?" "What's the story behind your belief?" When you sense a gap between what your partner is saying and what you're familiar with, that's the time to get clarity on what they're basing their statements on.

This is a prime mindset to learn more about the world and people other than yourself. After all, you can't assume that only your assumptions and beliefs are reasonable—everyone's are to some degree. So what is it that you are missing? Use questions that probe for meaning to find out.

3. Get all sides of the story. There are very few situations in life that are uncomplicated, cut-and-dried, or black and white. No matter how strongly someone feels about their particular viewpoint, there's always more than one side to a given story. By getting as much information as we possibly can about a certain topic, we delve deeper and understand more about the total nature of a situation, problem, or event.

This is often a case of not shutting out opinions or beliefs that might threaten or offend us, which in this day can be very difficult to do. But a responsibly asked question will help get a better picture of the greater context of things and will allow us to understand matters beyond our own limited view. "Is there another perspective on this situation?" "What are some of the things someone who disagrees with you would say?" "What would happen if someone did this differently?"

In general, don't be satisfied that you've gotten absolutely every fact of a certain matter to make an informed assumption. Imagine you are turning an idea over in your hands, looking at it from all sides. With just the right question, you can reveal a hidden aspect to the seemingly ordinary thing in front of you.

4. Ask follow-up questions. When we're trying to get close to someone, a lot of the questions we may ask of them don't have easy answers. In fact, if we were writing them out, they'd probably be more like two- or three-part questions with room to elaborate.

In personal interactions, we can emulate that depth—and show the strength of our focus—by asking follow-up questions. But they don't have to come immediately after your partner's answered. One author (me) suggests seeing how many questions you can ask in a row without offering any comment of your own, so you can allow your partner to expand their response and keep digging deeper.

Feed each question off the answer to the previous one. Pick up on one theme or idea and ask the other person to expand. Can they say more about this or that? Can they explain what they mean by this or that word or expression?

It's very important *not* to sound too much like a journalist or an inquisitor when asking follow-up questions. Instead, try to link your respondent's answers to things they've already discussed: "What you just mentioned about not fully understanding computer technology reminds me of what you said about not doing well in school. How do those relate?" or "How do you think that breakup affect your views on relationships?"

Questions are best when they aren't asking for plain old data, but require the other person to do a bit of analysis, to interpret, to connect two ideas or compare others. Good follow-up questions will make you sound invested in your partner's response, and actually engaging in the content itself. Yes, it may take a while for you to get to the answers you both need to know. But that's more time spent communicating.

5. Get comfortable with "dead air." People tend to be scared to death of "awkward silences"—those moments in conversation when there's a pregnant pause and nobody says anything. We tend to misinterpret these silences as a sign that either we or our partner has run out of things to say. Sometimes that's true. But sometimes, it's someone trying to gauge you and subtly seek permission to keep talking.

Thus, silence can work in communication's favor—when you're at ease with silence and don't rush to fill it yourself with inane chatter, you'll be prompting people to speak more and more. Think of it as seeing if moments of silence can help them generate their own, new thoughts and allow the conversation to get to a deeper level. If this is the case, all you have to do is keep quiet and let them take the conversation to the next level.

This is perhaps the easiest part of digging deeper; give people the space to do it for themselves instead of at your asking. Of course, sometimes people are pausing to gauge your reaction, or they're waiting for your approval or response. In this case, make some encouraging sounds or say something like, "go on" and see if they have more to say.

On the other hand, if they seem uncomfortable, it might genuinely be a case of a dying conversation. Laugh it off and try to pick it up again. Sometimes even great conversations spontaneously stall!

6. *Encourage your partner to come up with their own insights.* The best kinds of question-and-answer sessions aren't just one way, with one person providing insight and information to the other. It's always best—and far more conducive to good communication—when *everyone's* learning new things. Imagine you are both on a journey of discovery, helping one another uncover interesting new insights.

Questions that encourage self-discovery are, without exception, far more productive than questions that originate from a specific point of view. "What did you learn from that experience navigating the Amazon River? What do you think it added to your life?" Or perhaps "What would you want to say to your father if he were still alive?"

Like all questions, those intended to promote self-discovery need to be carefully considered. You never want to sound like you're on an inquisition, and it's easy to fall into that trap without trying. Especially with interpersonal relationships, you need to strike that balance of getting information while being supportive. If that strikes you as being too accommodating to someone's feelings—well, maybe personal relationships just aren't for you.

Fortunately, going deep doesn't necessarily have to be so direct as asking "What is your deepest fantasy and wildest dream?" Even the techniques we just discussed about asking questions aren't always applicable or helpful.

As important as that step is, it can be exhausting. It can also be *exhaustive*—theoretically, once you've talked about events and subjects only pertinent to your own lives, you'll run out of things to discover about yourself and the other person. There are only so many high school proms, parental arguments, complicated work scenarios, and family reunions you'll get in one life. In the worst-case scenario, it will turn into a job interview gone awry.

We are, of course, generally disposed to talk about ourselves and the things we've directly experienced or shared. But there's a considerable amount of insight to be obtained by discussing subjects and events external to your life. Author Daniel Menaker straightforwardly calls this approach turning the conversation toward "third things—not me, not them, but something else." It's not about you or the other person in particular.

It's just about something external, even as benign as the news of the day or the types of ferns you are surrounded by. Call it upgraded small talk.

Talking about these external topics serves as an inroad to discovering how somebody thinks and what they value. All this requires is that you ask how people feel about or would react to certain events, things, or situations.

If you directly ask someone personal details about themselves, their answers are often flat or inadequate. Imagine someone (other than a therapist) asking, "Tell me about when you feel angry," or "What do you believe in?" In addition to just sounding like left-field questions, they're not likely to elicit very lucid responses. Some might find the inquiries a bit intrusive or nosy, especially in the early stages of a friendship or interaction.

When you bring up things that are happening in the world, you actually *get* answers to those questions through others' reactions to those external situations. Their opinions and feedback offer clues to the way they really are without feeling on-the-spot or awkward. Discussing external things can help you get a more complete picture of what makes up the person you're with, and this is exceptionally helpful because there's no limit to what you can talk about. For an example of the type of deeper information you can glean indirectly, consider asking someone, "Where do you get your news? What kind of publications do you read most of the time?"

It's an innocent question, and it's something external. Yet you can learn much about someone's views, preferences, values, and overall worldview by knowing their reference sources and preferred viewpoints. This is useful far beyond any political purpose—you immediately understand how someone likes to see the world when you know what media they tend to consume.

Instead of digging deep directly, which is often off-putting or awkward at best, you can obtain a deeper perspective by measuring people's reactions to external things. You'll often get a more honest answer, and you'll learn more about them in the process.

Asking questions: not only does it take away your responsibility to talk all the time and help you find common ground with your conversational partner, but it also makes the other person feel like you care about them. Asking a question helps them see that their opinions and experiences matter to you, which makes them feel important. The secret sauce is simple; just ask questions and pay close attention to people's answers.

Takeaways:

- Going deeper and being better—this is about how we can enter into the type of interactions that we know are more beneficial for our happiness and mental well-being. How can we get into someone's good graces and let them feel good enough about us to let their guards down and build an actual relationship?
- The most obvious way to have people lower their guards is to pay them compliments early and often. Compliments are positive in general, but there are specific compliments that really impact the recipients. You should seek to compliment people on things they have made a conscious choice about and that reflect their thinking process. This gives them validation in a way that complimenting them on their eyes simply doesn't. These types of compliments subtly tell others that you agree with them on deep levels, and they can feel great that they have made a correct set of decisions.
- Sometimes people will lower their guards without even intending to if they find a

kind ear that's willing to listen intently and let them voice their inner thoughts. Listening is a skill that should be taught from childhood, but it's not, so we are left with all sorts of ineffective listening habits. We are all also naturally self-absorbed, which highlights the importance of listening as a skill to make others feel good about an interaction. While there are various methods to listen better, having a listening mindset is by far the most important part: it's not about you, focus on the other person, and if they said something, there's a reason—explore that.

- Of course, the tried and true way of directly getting deeper with people is to ask better questions. The simple truth is that most questions we use are surface level, and thus will only return surface-level responses. Here are a few guidelines for more piercing questions that will create more fertile ground for real substance: ask open-ended questions (don't ask for facts, ask for the analysis and reaction associated with the facts), go beyond assumptions (what are you missing in your own analysis?), get all sides of the story (the more perspectives the better), use follow-up questions (don't interject your own thoughts), get comfortable with dead air and in fact utilize it, and encourage people to come up with their own insights (so how did that change your opinion on things?).

Chapter 6. Looking Inwards

Jeffrey usually has a lot to say. He reads the news every morning and always seems to be consuming media whenever he has free time. He avoids gossip sites and reality television, but he generally learns a few facts each day. No wonder he can connect and relate with people on just about any topic that comes up.

Furthermore, he is able to offer his perspectives on the topic. Jeffrey is a blast to talk to because he always seems to be on the same page, and if he's not, he is willing to be curious and learn.

Other people might just answer with one-word replies and not provide insight or analysis. People like Mike, for example, who has a very narrow range of interests. Mike doesn't read much or keep up with current events and, if he's honest, he finds hobbies that aren't his own irrelevant and a little boring. Mike doesn't really like talking to people he doesn't already agree with, hasn't travelled much, and can get a bit argumentative with people who are very different from him.

You can be Jeffrey or you can be Mike. What's the difference? Jeffrey is a fabulous conversationalist because of his ability to discuss different opinions and perspectives. He's not just putting on an act; he is genuinely a curious person who thirsts for knowledge, information, and varying viewpoints. He has intentionally exposed himself to more of the world, and the more he learns, the less he feels he knows.

Mike, on the other hand, doesn't really enjoy other perspectives, different ideas, or new information—in other words, he's awful at conversation and socializing in general. Mike and Jeffrey go to prove something simple: people who are *interested* are often *interesting*. In other words, people who actively engage with life are always going to a) be more interesting to talk to and b) find other people interesting.

Become a person with lots of experiences and

lots to say. A more succinct way to put it is this that you should become the type of person you would like to get to know. You prefer someone who actively skydives over someone who watches television all day. You prefer someone who has something to teach you in an interesting subject. You prefer someone who displays passion and has opinions on a wide range of topics. Are you this person?

It's easy to think about other people in terms of what they bring to the conversational table, but what about *you*—are you cultivating the kind of personality that makes other people excited and interested in conversing with you? This question is more pronounced when you considering different people's attitudes to dating. Some are focused on whether they like the person in front of them, without sparing a thought for whether they are doing what they can to be likeable!

We might realize that in trying to create our conversation résumé, it is suspiciously empty or devoid of anything interesting. We might realize that we actually didn't do anything the past week besides work and eat. We might realize that when others share their new discoveries, we have literally nothing to add. Could this be behind your dread of small talk?

Therefore, the first section of this chapter focuses on looking inwards and becoming someone it's hard to *not* have a captivating conversation with. Although all of the techniques in this book are effective and useful, if you are the type of person with a lot to share and engage on, you will naturally overlap with them quite a bit.

Build Thyself

Conversation-worthy people actively pursue what they want. Sitting at home, working 24/7, or always talking about the same things won't make you interesting. In fact, it makes you seem like you have nothing going on in your life, and that may be an accurate assessment. Everyone has everyday experiences they aren't interested in rehashing with others. Most likely, when people ask you what you have been up to, they don't want to hear you say "work."

They may laugh and smile, but the conversation stops there because they know any other details from you will probably be boring. But imagine how you could lead the conversation into outrageous twists and turns if you said something else, like "I went skydiving. It was so exhilarating, dropping fourteen thousand feet through the air! My chute almost didn't deploy but it finally did—phew!"

Imagine the questions and comments people would have—but the point here is that you cared enough to take initiative and pursue an interest of yours, not that you are bragging about something you did. The point is that you went out and pursued a passion or interest. That's a worthy trait, and it results in more engagement and people taking interest in *you*. If someone asked you about your weekend, and your honest answers provoke those types of responses in people, then you're on the right track.

Maybe jumping out of planes is not your cup of tea—that's fine, too. You just need to find things that you have an interest in and take steps toward quenching that interest. You can later impart new knowledge to people, or you might find people who share the hobby and want to do it with you in the future.

The more interests you have, the more interesting you become. When you're engaged, you're engaging. These adages don't just sound clever; they ring true. People take an interest in those doing worthwhile things with their lives. You are also more likely to find someone who shares one or more of your hobbies. If you just have one single hobby, people will quickly find you boring because the odds of them sharing that interest are somewhat slim and because you offer little to talk about.

Imagine if all you talked about was collecting *Star Wars* action figures. Other than the occasional fanatic who also shares your hobby, most people won't be able to relate and won't find your conversation very interesting. They will like you less and avoid you when they realize that 1970s mint-condition Darth Vader dolls are all that you talk about, and thus they cannot relate to you on any level or find things to discuss with you that they care about.

But if you also are into painting, you can find more people who enjoy that, and you can appeal to a larger demographic of people because you don't just have that one single odd hobby that few others share with you. You're simply increasing your surface area of being interesting and engaging.

This all carries into the idea that you should avoid being one-dimensional. Avoid having so narrow a life that people find it difficult to connect with or understand you. I once had a boss whose sole interest, purpose, and passion in life was sports. That's it. The guy couldn't carry conversation like a normal person unless the topic related to sports. Or if the conversation was not about sports, he'd go out of his way to make sure it slowly became that way.

This put off people who didn't like or care about sports. It also prevented him from getting involved in conversations that didn't involve sports, which limited what he could talk about and who he could talk to. Most people felt annoyed by him, and even people who liked sports found his extremism obnoxious, annoying, and off-putting. Avoid being like my boss.

Always try to have something you are working on or toward—a project in your free time unrelated to work and unrelated to passive consumption of media via some type of screen. You don't have to set the bar to loving a passion, but rather just investigating something you are interested in. When you are actively looking forward to something, it's hard not to convey some of that excitement to others.

You will enjoy life more, learn a lot, and have more to talk about. Others will want to talk about your project and ask questions. Your new endeavor might also expose you to new people who share this passion, allowing you to broaden your social horizons.

In the movie *Yes Man*, Jim Carrey is forced to start saying yes to everything—literally everything. As a result, his life is transformed and he has many unforgettable experiences that he would never have had otherwise. He meets the love of his life, goes on many adventures, and other such things. Well, you need to be like his character and get into the habit of just saying yes and never saying no.

Cease the overthinking and giving yourself excuses to say no. You don't even need a reason to say yes, so saying yes should become very easy and automatic for you. Simply ask "Why not?" to kill the overthinking and go along with a new experience. Don't set expectations for what happens. Just be curious about what will take place and maintain an open mind.

Remember, for our purposes, you are truly becoming an interesting conversationalist if you have these experiences in your back pocket. It has to be *genuine*.

Branch Out

I'll never forget a child who sat down next to me at an old job and said, "Do you know what an elephant's pubic hair is called? It's called a dude." (I later found out this was an accurate fact.) The same concept comes into play in any conversation or interaction with a new person. You don't necessarily need to know and learn more for the sake of shocking people with new facts, but it is undeniably beneficial to how people view you. The more you know, the more you can talk about, and the more ways you can connect.

Whereas the prior point was on doing more, this idea emphasizes educating yourself more—proactively gaining knowledge instead of relying on it to come to you passively.

And it's not just fun animal facts—it's about perspectives, deeper understandings on a range of interesting and relevant topics. Be more well-read. You would be amazed what you can learn from books or even just newspapers five minutes a day. Being able to explain how things work, how things relate to each other, or what unique phenomena are enlightens others and makes you more interesting.

When others speak, you can listen and offer a fresh or supporting perspective, or connect their idea to yours. You can both leave the interaction feeling enriched. If you have little to say, though, that means you need to consume more in general and gain perspective outside of your everyday existence. (Here, we are reminded of the virtues of listening again…)

The more you have to talk about, the better. This does not mean that you ought to be starting a conversation with someone and running through a handful of topics one after another, but the more knowledgeable you are about different things, the better the chances are that you and your conversation partner will connect and see eye-to-eye on something.

You want to aim for breadth and touch on many topics as opposed to delving deeply into one sole topic. The act of knowing is more than simply being interesting—it makes conversation with you easy and, oftentimes, a delight. It allows you to teach, instruct, enlighten, lead, and always have something interesting to say.

Develop and share opinions, even if you have to start by parroting other people's opinions.

People love discussing their perspectives. Even if you disagree with someone, conversation follows. Without an opinion, conversation stalls and dies.

An opinion shows that you are interested, that you have made some sort of decision based on the facts you have, and that you are active in thinking about the world as a whole. Just imagine how frustrating it is to ask someone where they want to eat for dinner, but they never have an answer. Don't be that person.

Imagine this. You bring up Brexit and you expect the other person to respond to you about it. But the other person has nothing to say. With a shrug, all he says is "Oh, yeah, I heard about that." His lack of an opinion where you expect one freezes the conversation. There is nothing else to talk about, as that topic has been killed and now you don't want to start a new topic because you are afraid he will shoot that one down, too. You would be far more interested if you met someone who had a clear opinion on Brexit and was able to discuss it with you. A lack of opinion simply makes it seem like you don't think about things.

On the other hand, imagine you're talking

with someone and bring up the topic of Brexit, and all of a sudden, the other person launches off into a diatribe about their (very strong) opinion, more or less preaching about why they're right and everyone else isn't. When you ask a question or disagree, you get dismissed or "educated" on the right way to think.

Good conversationalists know that it's better to use opinions to drive conversation and connection, rather than shut it down or create division. They are not afraid of disagreement or difference; rather, they explore it with genuine curiosity. In other words, having an opinion per se is not enough—you need to be broad-minded, flexible and able to hear other people's opinions, too.

Not everyone has had tons of life experience or exposure to the news. But everyone has the ability to be curious about new things and desire to learn. Having the curiosity to care about other people and new things will make others want to talk to you and explain things to you or teach you new ideas. Every conversation is a chance to learn something new, if you have the right mindset.

Intellectual curiosity compels you to explore

the world, both what's right around you, and the world far away from you that requires a sixteen-hour flight or more to explore. You don't have to fly to another country to learn a new language, meet new people, and try exotic food. From home, you can broaden your horizons, become more engaged in the world around you, and thus become more interesting. All you need to do is take the first step and learn. Bring this attitude to your conversations, and you can't help but be a great person to talk to.

At the same time it must be said, doing more and knowing more isn't a panacea.

You could be the most interesting person in the world, but no one will care if you engage in conversational habits that, for lack of a better word, *repulse* people. Indeed, as you might have seen in your daily life, sometimes it's an overall net gain if you don't have to deal with people who annoy the heck out of you, no matter how much of a benefit they represent. It's not a stretch to propose that you'd highly prefer someone who was milquetoast yet not irritating or frustrating.

In other words, appearing benign and non-annoying will probably make you a better conversationalist than being someone who is actually interesting but has frustrating interpersonal habits. Thankfully, we have learned a multitude of conversational tactics to make you appealing and captivating—now let's make sure you're not exhibiting toxic habits and behaviors. These include:

You Only See Black and White

Put another way, you only see *one* correct way of doing things, and anything that diverges from that view is wrong. And the right way happens to be your view. What does that mean? Well, if you're right and already know it all, there's no point to talking to anyone to find out something new, is there?

This is a rather large caveat to the prior section's credo of branching out and developing more opinions and thoughts on issues. That still rings true, but you must express yourself while respecting and honoring the perspectives of other people. Most importantly, don't make them feel judged, attacked, or lesser-than when you do express yourself. It's not just a small talk or conversation tip, it's a lesson for life.

If you only see one way of doing things, if you are constantly governed by "should" and "must" and if you typically assume people are "stupid" or "blind" then you, sir or madam, are judgmental. When you are judgmental, this means you are jumping to a conclusion, and almost always a negative one, without taking life circumstances, opinions, and preferences into account. You assume the worst, usually, and it is based only on your limited perspective and life experience and imposing it onto other people (should or must). If they don't conform, then suddenly they gain the title of "stupid" or "blind."

Being judgmental isn't all bad. When our inner judge is alerted, we are able to make clear decisions and avoid potentially dangerous situations. Being judgmental also helps us to be creative, clever, and insightful. But for most of us, it's a fairly thin line, and we can easily verge into offensive territory. Outside of only a few contexts, judgment actually holds very little use for us (certainly it is detrimental in the social context). Which of the below apply to you?

- You can't see people beyond their perceived flaws.
- You struggle to see the positive in others.
- You jump to conclusions first, then analyze later (if at all).

- You don't think in terms of ambiguity or shades of gray; there is only black or white.
- You are intolerant of people who come to different conclusions than you.

Whether you are doing it by expressing yourself, or dismissing the opinions and thoughts of others, this type of behavior can be truly hurtful and damaging to others. You might think you're open-minded, but if you only have criticisms and judgments of others, you're probably not. Your mindset will be reflected in the way you engage socially. What you don't want is to treat conversations as mere opportunities to prove yourself right, to boast, to win arguments, to show off or to feel superior. Judgment is the opposite of open curiosity and playfulness. It narrows our perception, shuts down our compassion and gets in the way of our creativity. And more than that, it's pretty damn boring!

Just as you wouldn't want to be put in a box the moment you talk to people, others also don't respond all that well to feeling as if they're being judged. This is a hard habit to break because opinions can easily become personal. When you act this way, you tend to offend people and make them feel like they can't express themselves around you.

Sadly, some overly combative people really do think that life is about finding the right answer, clinging to it forever, and beating other people over the head when they're "wrong." In short, you become a full-fledged, card-carrying, badge-wearing member of the *Belief Police. Open the door! You're wrong about something!* A Belief Policeman makes it his or her duty to let others know when they are wrong, and make sure they are thinking in the same way as them.

A Belief Policeman might be very effective at imposing their beliefs on others, but this habit is going to make you downright obnoxious to talk to. Who wants to spend time with someone who makes them feel judged, attacked, and defensive? So people stop opening up to you and will eventually avoid you altogether. Little by little, this will aggregate into a sense of unease and discomfort around you, and at that point, people will just start to avoid you.

There's a small chance that they might agree with some of the negative things you are saying, but that still doesn't make them feel safe around you. Eventually, they'll just avoid you so they can sidestep the feeling of having to censor themselves.

Being Belief Policemen causes us to spend way too much time squabbling over things just because we feel that other people believe or think something different than we do and must be corrected. But at what cost does this come? And in the end, does it really matter? Couples' counselors often tell people: do you want to be right or do you want to be happy? Sounds dramatic but it's pretty true, I think. Does it matter if you are "technically correct" about something, but you've alienated all your friends to prove that point?

This is especially true when it comes to matters of taste and opinion. These are completely subjective. What looks good to you might be completely ugly to another person. You won't convince anyone to like chocolate more than they already do or to enjoy beets when they hate them, so it's really a waste of your time—and an extremely annoying one at that—to exert your energy trying to convince them.

If you feel that someone is doing something wrong, or thinking something wrong, instead of making that assumption, take a step back and wonder if you simply don't have enough information yourself. If somebody has an opinion, respect that they have a reasonable basis for that opinion. After all, no one thinks their own decisions and thoughts are stupid. Ask questions about how they came up with that idea and what information and assumptions they hold.

You might just learn something. For instance, if someone drives into a parking spot that you were quite clearly waiting for, you might be tempted to think that they are just an inconsiderate and rude person. However, suppose that the person stumbles out of the car and falls to the ground, screaming that they are having a heart attack. Might your assessment of the situation change ever so slightly?

You've probably done some things other people might find bizarre, but there was a perfectly rational reason for your actions, right? I'm sure you would have preferred others to try and better understand your position rather than jump in to argue with you.

Extend the courtesy of that assumption to others. Give people the benefit of the doubt. At least assume they have reasonable underpinnings for their opinions and beliefs. What experiences have they had in their lives that might explain why they hold a position in such contrast to yours? Remember that people have their own reasons for opinions and beliefs and that not everybody thinks just the way you do. You can either recognize this or not.

Pushing this even further, what if you delve deeper into someone's opinions, beliefs or tastes and find that you really can't agree or understand? Let's be honest, you've probably encountered somebody with an opinion that made you scratch your head, to say the least. Here's the thing though: a great conversationalist can always find *some* common ground, can be respectful, lighthearted, curious and kind...without agreeing in the least with their conversation partner. It's all about prioritizing enjoyable human connection over the need to agree or be right.

Hopefully, this is a mindset that will lead to a more natural type of curiosity about others— if only to see what pieces of information you are missing. If you can model an accepting and mature attitude even with those you have a little friction with, you may even find you develop a stronger kind of connection with them. It's a very impressive and attractive thing to be able to spend time with someone and say, "look, we don't agree, but so what?

Tell me more about such-and-such..."

If all else fails, try to recognize that everyone is doing the best they can, the smartest they can, and the nicest they can, with the circumstances they were dealt. It's only when we feel that people are not doing their best or trying hard that our judgmental instincts arise. If we instead take the perspective that everyone is making their greatest effort, suddenly things change.

Overall, choose your battles and don't fret about the small details of what you can't change. You'll be happier and less stressed, and you'll notice a direct, positive correlation between that and the quality of your friendships and interactions.

Takeaways:

- This book is littered with tips and tricks to make small talk less painful and flow more smoothly. It's been almost all outwardly focused—on the other person, on the interaction, and on what you can say to improve your social exchanges. While that's ultimately the most important part, there remains a vital part of the equation left for the end: looking inwards to yourself. From the perspective of others, are you someone who is easy to make small talk with? Are you someone who energizes and makes people curious, or are you rather a drain on their precious energy? We have to make sure that our input is proportional to the type of output we want.

- Build thyself and they will come. Not really, but the point is to truly look at yourself and ask what is interesting. What are you really doing with your life? Are you the type of person others would want to meet and interact with? If yes, then your conversation résumé better show it. If no, then it's time to take action and build yourself. Pursue what you are interested in, actively engage in life, and find passions or hobbies. Would you rather meet someone who surfs and dives recreationally, or someone who only watches television on weekends? *The more interests you have, the more interesting you become* and *when you're engaged, you're engaging.*

- In a similar vein, learn more, read more, expose yourself to more, and think more. Stop relying on information to passively come to you; proactively learn about what you are interested in. Have intellectual curiosity. Develop opinions by thinking through different perspectives and become more knowledgeable in general. These two points make you the type of person with whom free-flowing conversation happens naturally, and doesn't have to be manufactured.

- With that said, you could be the most interesting person in the world and no one will care if you have one of the most repulsive social habits: being judgmental. This is when you only see in black and white, and everyone falls into two categories: your perspective, or the wrong one. You are a member of the Belief Police. You can bet that this is annoying and frustrating to others, to the point where it will eventually lead to them feeling unsafe around you and outright avoiding you. When you are feeling an urge to judge, try to instead take the perspective that you lack the information to make a smart judgment, and become more curious about others and what you are missing. If all else fails, make the assumption that everyone is simply trying their best with what they have.

Summary Guide

CHAPTER 1. UGH, SMALL TALK

- We are a social species, and multiple studies confirm this. Lack of social interaction itself is harmful, and for our purposes, lack of *substantive* social interaction is no better. Gaining the ability and skill to fast-forward through small talk has incredible value for the relationships in your life—old and future. However, before we jump into conversation tactics, it's helpful to start before we actually meet and greet someone. How can we prepare beforehand to have consistently great small talk and interactions? In many ways, it turns out.
- There are a couple of ways we can get ready for small talk and warm up, so to speak. The two approaches are what you might assume: physiologically, and psychologically. Psychological preparation is a matter of getting in the mood to socialize and also becoming used to

initiating interaction. This can be done with "ten-second relationships," which plunge you into the deep end if only for a moment. The idea is to start small and short, with low expectations, and build from there. You'll eventually see that it's easy and quite safe—you might even find it to be enjoyable, and frequently want to extend past ten seconds.

- Physically, you should seek to warm up by reading out loud before socializing and making sure you exaggerate emotional expressiveness and variation. Read a passage out loud three times and notice the difference in engagement, and you can instantly see the contrast in how you might come across. You should act like a teacher reading to grade school-aged children, and run through the whole gamut of emotions, expressions, and voices. Go over the top. This is meant to warm you up, as well as bring awareness to how lacking in expressiveness you probably are on a normal basis.
- An additional way of preparing before conversations is to get your own information and life in order, and this can be done by following a conversation résumé. The purpose is to draw into your past and find what makes you an interesting person, and make sure that is

all at the tip of your tongue for easy usage. We often forget what we can bring to a conversation, and this lack of available topics adds a sense of stress and avoidance.

- We all dislike small talk, but it does have a role. Getting to know someone happens in a sequential manner, and we cannot skip steps if we want to go deeper. It can be said that there are four stages to an interaction, and small talk is the first, followed by fact disclosure, then opinion disclosure, then emotion disclosure. The sequence can be played with, but understanding small talk's role is important.

CHAPTER 2. INITIAL IMPRESSIONS

- What determines whether you hit it off with someone? It's not circumstantial; rather, it's a matter of you taking charge and setting the tone to be friendly and open. Most people treat others like strangers and thus won't become friends. So change that script from the very beginning, put people at ease and let them be comfortable around you.
- The first way to set the tone is to speak like friends: topic-wise, tone-wise, and even privacy-wise. People will go along

with the tone you set as long as you aren't outright offensive. A powerful aspect of this is showing emotion as friends do, instead of filtering yourself and putting up a wall for the literal purpose of keeping people insulated at a distance. And stop being so darned literal and serious. A conversation does not have to be about sharing facts, and some comments can be used solely for the purpose of seeing how the other person will react.

- Another aspect of setting the right tone is to search for similarities and also allow the opportunity to create them. When people observe similarity, they instantly open up and embrace it because it is a reflection of themselves. There are only good assumptions and connotations, so we should actively seek them out. You can do this by digging more deeply into people's lives and asking questions to find seemingly unrelated similarities, divulging more information yourself, and also mirroring them physically. Also, don't discount the value of *mutual dislike*—it's not negative to talk about negative things, per se.

- Finally, even if you follow these steps, sometimes people either aren't willing to engage or not good at opening up themselves. You can blast past this by using forms of *elicitation*, in which you put forth a topic or question in a way that a person will feel compelled to engage or elaborate. These take the form of prompting the person to reply to your recognition, encouraging mutual complaining, assisting your naiveté, and correcting your incorrect assumption or information.

CHAPTER 3. HOW TO BE CAPTIVATING

- Captivating people usually refers to telling a story that leaves them listening like children (in a good way). Storytelling is a big topic that is often made overly complex, but there are many ways of creating this feeling in small, everyday ways. To captivate others is no easy feat, but the material and ability lies within all of us. We just have to know where it is and how to access it.
- An easy way to imagine everyday storytelling is that your life is a series of stories—mini-stories, to be exact. Instead of giving one-word answers, get into the habit of framing your answers as a story with a point. It creates more engagement, lets you show your personality, and allows for smoother conversation. The bonus here is that you can prepare these

before a conversation.

- The 1:1:1 method of storytelling is to simplify it as much as possible. The impact of a story won't necessarily be stronger if it is ten sentences versus two sentences. Therefore, the 1:1:1: method focuses on the discussion and reaction that occurs after a story. A story can be composed solely of (1) one action, (2) one emotion to be evoked, and (3) a one-sentence summary. Don't get lost rambling, and also make sure your listener feels that they are fully participating in the conversation.

- The story spine is more or less the formula for every movie that exists. It's a simple framework that you can use in your everyday stories and conversations, because it teaches you what emotional beats exist in a story. There is the status quo, the event that kicks things off, the set of consequences for changing the status quo, the climax or resolution, and then what happens after the fact.

- Stories can also be the basis for an inside joke. When you think about it, an inside joke is something that comes up multiple times with the same person and evokes a positive emotion. It's the same topic brought up in a different context. Thus, you just need to call back to a story through a conversation and there's a good chance it will stick as a "Remember when we talked about..." moment. The more you use it, the more a unique bond is created between only the two of you.

- Improving your storytelling ability is important, but what about eliciting stories from others? You can phrase your questions carefully to ask for stories rather than answers from people, which is a simple way to make conversation easier and more enjoyable for everyone involved. There are ways to make people open up to you and want to keep gabbing. Remember the lesson we learned with the 1:1:1 method in pinpointing the emotions that people are trying to evoke. To amplify this, you can *pin the tail on the donkey* and strategically add on to people's stories.

CHAPTER 4. KEEP IT FLOWING AND SMOOTH

- How can you keep conversation, small talk especially, flowing smoothly when you don't feel like you have anything to talk about? This is a challenge even with good friends sometimes. Most of the time, this feeling of stagnancy occurs because you are doing exactly that—stagnating—and nothing is being added or extracted from the interaction on either side. But there are several ways you can change that.

- First, create a sense of motion. Staying on the same topic, sentiment, or feeling for too long will create a feeling of boredom and even mild stress. *Why can't you escape it?* Indeed, if you watch a movie and it's just people talking the entire time, the movie better be *damn well written* to be interesting. To contrast, Joseph Campbell's hero's journey is a classic story that follow someone's quest, success, and subsequent transformation. Luckily, there are a multitude of ways to create motion in an interaction, but the most powerful part is simply realizing that things must move in some way.
- Sometimes, despite knowing full well that we must create motion, we are unable to do it. Sometimes our minds go blank. The next couple of sections deal with this specifically—how can you think more quickly on your feet? This requires practice; no one who manages it consistently is truly born with such a quick wit. And so how do you practice it? With free association, by simply taking a word and naming a few words or concepts that it reminds you of. The important part is to train your brain's quick response reflex and break through any mental filters you might possess. You can also

choose two words and relate them with a brief story, or flip to random words in the dictionary and use them to create a story.

- Finally, in case all else escapes your mind, there are three incredibly helpful acronyms that can assist you in never running out of things to say on the fly. These are: HPM, SBR, and EDR. HPM stands for History (your personal experience with the topic), Philosophy (your opinion on the topic), and Metaphor (what the topic makes you think of). SBR stands for Specific (more detail on the topic), Broad (broader context of topic), and Related (related topics). EDR stands for Emotion (the emotions the topic evokes in the other person), Detail (more detail on the topic), and Restatements (restating the topic to prompt greater elaboration).

CHAPTER 5. GO DEEPER, BE BETTER

- Going deeper and being better—this is about how we can enter into the type of interactions that we know are more beneficial for our happiness and mental well-being. How can we get into someone's good graces and let them feel good enough about us to let their guards down and build an actual relationship?

- The most obvious way to have people lower their guards is to pay them compliments early and often. Compliments are positive in general, but there are specific compliments that really impact the recipients. You should seek to compliment people on things they have made a conscious choice about and that reflect their thinking process. This gives them validation in a way that complimenting them on their eyes simply doesn't. These types of compliments subtly tell others that you agree with them on deep levels, and they can feel great that they have made a correct set of decisions.
- Sometimes people will lower their guards without even intending to if they find a kind ear that's willing to listen intently and let them voice their inner thoughts. Listening is a skill that should be taught from childhood, but it's not, so we are left with all sorts of ineffective listening habits. We are all also naturally self-absorbed, which highlights the importance of listening as a skill to make others feel good about an interaction. While there are various methods to listen better, having a listening mindset is by far the most important part: it's not about you, focus on the other person, and if they said something, there's a reason—explore

that.

- Of course, the tried and true way of directly getting deeper with people is to ask better questions. The simple truth is that most questions we use are surface level, and thus will only return surface-level responses. Here are a few guidelines for more piercing questions that will create more fertile ground for real substance: ask open-ended questions (don't ask for facts, ask for the analysis and reaction associated with the facts), go beyond assumptions (what are you missing in your own analysis?), get all sides of the story (the more perspectives the better), use follow-up questions (don't interject your own thoughts), get comfortable with dead air and in fact utilize it, and encourage people to come up with their own insights (so how did that change your opinion on things?).

CHAPTER 6. LOOKING INWARDS

- This book is littered with tips and tricks to make small talk less painful and flow more smoothly. It's been almost all outwardly focused—on the other person, on the interaction, and on what you can say to improve your social exchanges. While that's ultimately the most important part, there remains a vital part of the equation left for the end: looking inwards to yourself. From the perspective of others, are you someone who is easy to make small talk with? Are you someone who energizes and makes people curious, or are you rather a drain on their precious energy? We have to make sure that our input is proportional to the type of output we want.

- Build thyself and they will come. Not really, but the point is to truly look at yourself and ask what is interesting. What are you really doing with your life? Are you the type of person others would want to meet and interact with? If yes, then your conversation résumé better show it. If no, then it's time to take action and build yourself. Pursue what you are interested in, actively engage in life, and find passions or hobbies. Would you rather meet someone who surfs and dives recreationally, or someone who only watches television on weekends? *The more interests you have, the more interesting you become* and *when you're engaged, you're engaging.*

- In a similar vein, learn more, read more, expose yourself to more, and think more. Stop relying on information to passively come to you; proactively learn about what you are interested in. Have intellectual curiosity. Develop opinions by thinking through different perspectives and become more knowledgeable in general. These two points make you the type of person with whom free-flowing conversation happens naturally, and doesn't have to be manufactured.

- With that said, you could be the most interesting person in the world and no one will care if you have one of the most repulsive social habits: being judgmental. This is when you only see in black and white, and everyone falls into two categories: your perspective, or the wrong one. You are a member of the Belief Police. You can bet that this is annoying and frustrating to others, to the point where it will eventually lead to them feeling unsafe around you and outright avoiding you. When you are feeling an urge to judge, try to instead take the perspective that you lack the information to make a smart judgment, and become more curious about others and what you are missing. If all else fails, make the assumption that everyone is simply trying their best with what they have.